D1302295

Women, power, and politics

TAVISTOCK WOMEN'S STUDIES

Women, power, and politics

MARGARET STACEY
and MARION PRICE

TAVISTOCK PUBLICATIONS
LONDON AND NEW YORK

First published in 1981 by
Tavistock Publications Ltd
11 New Fetter Lane,
London EC4P 4EE

Published in the USA by
Tavistock Publications
in association with Methuen, Inc.
733 Third Avenue, New York,
NY 10017

© 1981 Margaret Stacey and
Marion Price

Typeset by Inforum Ltd,
Portsmouth
Printed in Great Britain by
Richard Clay (The Chaucer Press),
Ltd, Bungay, Suffolk

British Library Cataloguing in
Publication Data

Stacey, Margaret
  Women, power, and politics. –
  (Social science paperbacks;
  153).
  1. Women in politics
  I. Title   II. Price, Marion
  III. Series
  329   HQ1236   80–41723
  ISBN 0–422–76140–0
  ISBN 0–422–76150–8 Pbk

ISBN 0 422 76140 0
hardback
ISBN 0 422 76150 8
paperback

Contents

Changes in Politics and Power?

> Vote, vote, vote for Mr Wilson
> Here comes Katie at the door
> Katie is the one that we like best
> So we don't want Mr Wilson any more.
> Walk out!

A girls' singing game collected by Kate Stacey in Brynmill Junior School, Swansea in the early 1960s.

> Vote, vote, vote for little Sharon,
> In comes Rachel at the door, at the door
> Rachel is a lady
> And she wants to have a baby
> So we don't want Sharon any more.
> Push her out!

> Vote, vote, vote for little Rachel,
> In comes Marika at the door, at the door
> Marika is a lady and she wants a little baby
> So we don't want Rachel any more.
> Push her out!

Collected by her daughter Rachel Stacey at the Sherrier School, Lutterworth in 1979.

Preface

There are many we must thank for their help in the production of this book. Marion wishes to thank her family and friends, without whose encouragement and support her part in this book would not have been possible. She owes a special debt of gratitude to students and colleagues who have shared their ideas and experiences with her and sustained her efforts with their friendship and enthusiasm. Finally, her thanks are due to Mike for trying to understand.

Meg wishes to record certain personal debts. First, to her parents who, fresh from the struggle for the vote, reared her from the outset to be aware of feminism. To her mother, who, while herself accepting a predominantly domestic role, made Meg aware of continued discrimination against women in the public domain; to her father, who had been a militant feminist, who first alerted her to the need for a radical redivision of labour between the sexes in the private domain as well as in the public domain, and who, more than many men of his period, practised what he preached. Her more recent debts are to her family of marriage, to her friends, to colleagues (particularly those working on the sociology of health and illness) and students, especially the postgraduates, in the Sociology Department at Warwick University, and to her sisters in the women's movement. She doubts whether she could have survived a concerted spell of personal bereavement and adversity to write her part of the book at all had it not been for their help. Personally she wishes to thank Jo and Olive Banks, Margot Jefferys, and Richard Turner (who, sadly, has since died), Olive Stevens, Virginia Olesen, Elizabeth Wilson, Hilary Rose, and Hilary Graham. Meg's special debts are to two groups of people: her family and her sisters in the women's movement. She has already referred to her family of origin. Her five children, despite their own overwhelming grief, offered unfailing practical and psychological support. They were and are a living reminder of all that is best in the social institution of marriage and the family, both of which come in for a good deal of criticism in the pages that follow. The support from sisters in Britain and abroad – those who understood only at second hand as well as those who understood at first hand (including women in the village Women's Institute and in the British Sociological Association women's caucus) – betokened a love and solidarity which she felt almost physically.

Personal suffering, death, and bereavement are too rarely discussed in our society: acknowledgements to those who help therefore are too rarely made. For this reason Meg has chosen to make this public acknowledgement, *mores* notwithstanding. She makes it also because it is relevant to what has become a central theme of this book: how can the best qualities that have traditionally been connected with the family and seen as feminine, tenderness, caring, support, be preserved and enhanced as women move into the public domain, claiming and receiving equality alongside men?

Meg also wishes to record how much she owes to Frank, who, although he was no feminist, was always liberal, loving, loyal, and supportive and without whom she might not have learned how to write at all.

We both wish to thank Terri Moss for the typing and Penny

Buckle for all that she did in the Warwick Office to help the production.

We also wish to thank the librarians and information officers at the City of Liverpool College of Higher Education, Warwick University, the Women's Research and Resources Centre, and the Equal Opportunities Commission. Their help in our searches was invaluable.

Margaret Stacey
Marion Price
April, 1980

ONE

Introduction

When we were asked to write this book the question that was set was: 'Why is it, when women have had the vote for fifty years, so few women are to be found in politically powerful positions?' After we had thought about this question for a while and surveyed the evidence we concluded that the question had to be turned on its head. It became: 'How can it possibly have come about in so short a period of time that so many women have become involved in politics?' Given that there are so few women in powerful or even influential public positions this may seem surprising, for it is true, as Helga Nowotny put it: 'where power is, women are not' (1980 : 147). It is undoubtedly true that the great hopes of the suffragettes have not been realized. Women have not emerged as equal partners with men in public life.

Our reasons for feeling that we have to explain why women have come so far, rather than explaining why there have been so

1

few gains, rest on two grounds. The first is that what women have been trying to do in the last two hundred years has been very radical and quite a new departure in social arrangements. They have been, for the first time in history, trying to achieve some independence as persons and to exercise some power as individuals in their own right. This is what in our view has been the really radical move, for we do not believe that women have always and everywhere been oppressed, as has often been suggested in the liberation movement, nor do we believe that women have never exercised power: that is patently not true. What does seem to be the case is that the political power that women have exercised in the past and in other societies has always derived from their position in a familial or kinship group. What women in the feminist movement did when they made a bid for the vote was to demand that women be treated as persons, as individuals, that the newly developing notions of individualism be applied to them as well as to all adult men. Our second reason is that when over fifty years ago full franchise on equal terms with men was granted to women, little else changed. No other social institutions changed, no other alterations were made in the division of labour; there was no change in the ideologies that supported the division of labour and the previously existing power structure. It is true that there had been certain antecedent changes which have helped women in their moves to political power. Thus, by the end of the nineteenth century married women had gained rights to their own property and income and women were beginning to get a foothold in hitherto exclusively male educational institutions and professions. Nevertheless, the ideology of what it was proper for women to do remained largely untouched. Women were still the gentle sex, their task was nurturant, caring, supportive; not for them the leadership roles. This ideology remained unchanged, we believe, because the institution of the family remained unchanged and the ideology was necessary for its legitimation and maintenance in that form. There were, of course, some changes in the family, most notably the decline in the size of the nuclear family and its increasing privatization. But the essential assumption that the major task of women was to serve a husband, bear and rear his children remained. With the development of contraception it began to be recognized that

2

some women could opt out of the mother role other than by remaining celibate. But it was never suggested that women having borne children, this being their unique capability, men might rear them. The well-to-do might hire other women to rear their children for them. This option was not open to the great majority of women, nor, except in times of war, were arrangements made on any considerable scale for the collective sharing of child-rearing.

Had we looked only at the formal political arena and confined our notions of power to that arena, we could not have reached our present conclusions, for we would not have thought to examine the evidence that we present in the pages that follow. We have asked the following kinds of questions: was there ever an age or a place where women ruled? If so, in what circumstances? Was there ever a place or time where women shared in political decisions equally with men? Is it true that where women have been shut away, as in societies with purdah, they have been powerless? Did women, do women, have power in the family? What kinds of power have women exercised? What are the origins of this power? How and in what circumstances did British women come to demand the vote? How did they come to see themselves as individuals? How powerful are women now and in what ways?

What do we mean by power? It is, as is well known, a difficult concept to define and has been approached differently by pluralist political scientists, Marxists, and sociologists. Power is clearly one element in all social relationships and is difficult to separate from such related concepts as authority, control, influence, and domination. There are problems as to the overt and covert exercise of power, and problems of the relationship between the exercise of power and the normative order in a stratified society. The notion of power undoubtedly has to do with the ability of an individual or a group to influence the course of events in the direction they desire even against resistance by others.

In thinking about power in relation to women, we, like Davidoff (1977) accept Lukes's view that power is an 'essentially contested' concept (Lukes 1974 : 9; Gallie 1955–56): what is power is essentially a matter of dispute. And, like Oakley (1974a), we have found valuable Worsley's distinction between two forms of politics: 'the exercise of constraint in any relationship', and 'the specialized machinery of government, together with the administrative apparatus of state and party organization' (Worsley 1964 : 17).

It has been the blindness of political scientists, looking only at this formal state apparatus, that has led to the 'why so few?' question being asked at all. As soon as the presence of power in all relationships between men and women is recognized and their articulation with the formal state apparatus examined, a completely new light is shed upon the whole issue. As Oakley has it, while the traditional wife-mother-housewife role 'is correlated with certain types of powerlessness, it also has its own avenues of influence' (1974a : 14). It is these, their relationship to power, the changes over time, and their relationship to formal politics that we examine in the pages that follow.

The notion of two domains, the public and the private, and its relevance for our problem was called to our attention by the works of Cynthia Nelson (1974), Rosaldo and Lamphere (1974), and Dorothy Smith (1974). Nelson points to 'the commonplace notion that the human universe is segregated [in the Middle East] into two social worlds marked out by the nature of the two sexes, (and) . . . characterized as being *private* (the women's) and *public* (the men's)' (1974 : 552, emphasis in original). But Nelson challenges, as we show in Chapter 2, the associated notion that women are therefore powerless, or 'unpolitical' in some sense. Rosaldo (Rosaldo and Lamphere 1974 : 23–4) refers to 'domestic' and 'public' orientations associated with the social roles of men and women in most societies, the women being identified with the former and the men with the latter, which she sees as 'the necessary framework for an examination of male and female roles in any society'. This notion is developed by Lamphere (Rosaldo and Lamphere 1974 : 97–112) who, to quote Rosaldo, shows that 'variations in domestic group structure are importantly related to variations in types of female power (Rosaldo and Lamphere 1974 : 35).

Dorothy Smith has found the distinction essential in her analysis. We came across it after we had developed our original notions but it is her conceptualization that best expresses our approach, for it is designed to take account of a variety of societies and a variety of historical periods.

4

'As political and economic modes of action are organized as differentiated structures external to people as individuals, their existence is bifurcated into "public" and "private" spheres. . . . The separation of public and private spheres is not a feature of all social forms. It does not exist in the smaller and technologically more primitive societies of the past and some other people's present. In our own past the first moment of externalization is political – a separation of the organization of political and military action. The second is an externalization of the productive process in the capitalist enterprise. . . . The public sphere is that sphere in which "history" is made. But the public sphere is also the sphere of male activity. Domestic activity becomes relegated to the private sphere, *and is mediated by men who move between both*. Women have only a place in the private, domestic sphere.' (Smith 1974 : 6, our emphasis)

Rosaldo (1980) in a later work has moved nearer to this position when she points out the dangers of using the notion of 'two spheres' in a sense that appears immutable and inevitable, a version which she shows is rooted in the values and ideologies of a particular form of male-dominated society and incorporated into anthropology (see Stacey 1980 for a similar analysis of sociological assumptions). Not only is the distinction between public and private domains historically specific, empirically and conceptually, the very nature of the domains themselves changes as we shall see.

Traditionally the concepts of power with which scholars have worked have come from the public domain, for they have been articulated in and about that domain (e.g. Dahl (1961), Polsby (1963), Blondel (1965), Stanworth and Giddens (1974), Urry and Wakeford (1973)). This is why women have been 'hidden from history' (Rowbotham 1973; Smith 1974); it is also why the conventional vocabularies of power of all the major schools seem inappropriate for the study of women's public status, indeed for their status at all. This applies particularly to those approaches where the exercise of power is identified in situations of conflicts of interest as revealed in the opposing policy preferences and actions of contending parties. Such analyses identify the powerful as those who prevail in cases of decision-making where there is observable conflict. They relate only to relatively few of the circumstances in which women's preferences have prevailed, as for example in the campaign for the franchise, in support of legislation affecting women's duties and conditions in the family, in employment, and in the matter of the control of their fertility. Such a behaviourist analysis leaves open to question the extent to which such successes represent significant victories: the legislation has not challenged notions of a woman's 'proper place'.

Nor can this approach explain the under-representation of women in 'politics proper'. According to this view, the conclusion must be not only that women do not exercise power in the public domain, but that they do not have interests that are harmed by the exercise of formal political power by a large preponderance of men, and that consequently these interests do not have to be expressed as claims on public policy. Women, then, are neither rulers nor ruled: they are simply invisible in the world of public affairs. The approach ends by restating what is in need of explanation: the under-representation of women in the public domain is outside the scope of political analysis.

The arguments of Bachrach and Baratz are informative so far as the analysis of women and politics is concerned. They have argued against the restricted definition of political relations used in behaviourist analysis and in favour of an approach that recognizes a 'second face of power' (Bachrach and Baratz 1970). Power is exercised, they argue, when some groups are prevented from raising issues that are inimical to the interests of the power holders, such topics are kept 'off the agenda' by the dominant group 'to the extent that a person or group – consciously or unconsciously – creates or reinforces barriers to the public airing of policy conflicts, that person or group has power' (1970 : 8). They thus extend the exercise of power to non-decision making as well as decision making. This argument would lead one to suggest that women's under-representation in the public political domain can be conceptualized not simply in terms of women's lack of interest in politics (the 'apathy' of the behaviourists) but of the ability of men to prevent (consciously or unconsciously) women's issues entering politics.

Many of the issues that women seek to raise, especially as they relate to an increase in practical autonomy for women (take the case of nursery or crèche provision, for example), are undoubtedly not in the interests of men. Increased autonomy for women threatens men not only by the increased competition from women seeking to enter the public domain, but also by a decline in the support and services that they expect as individuals from women in their families. What have generally been termed 'women's issues' are not taken up in mainstream debates, they are trivialized and seen as second-class issues, not of prime importance. One of the interesting things that has happened since the mid-seventies in Britain is that this agenda-making by men and the priorities within the agenda have begun to be challenged, as we argue in Chapter 7.

Bachrach and Baratz (1970) also allow for the notion that conflict may be 'covert' as well as 'overt' and that those who are relatively powerless in any relationship may be unwilling or unable to translate their interests into 'policy preferences'. The governed may have 'grievances' which do not become full-fledged demands on public policy. Moreover, both rulers and ruled may believe that some issues are not a matter for public controversy or concern. Women's issues commonly fall into such a category and it is therefore no wonder that much political controversy lacks salience for women (Goot and Reid 1975). While women's frustrations with politicians' ignorance of and indifference to their problems as housewives or mothers is well-known, it is more often the women who are accused of apathy and not understanding the rules of the political game – a neat case of 'victim-blaming', in which attempts are made to explain the political behaviour of one half of the population in terms of their 'deviance'. At the same time, right across the political spectrum, the parameters that define the boundaries of the 'political' remain unchallenged. Debates on the left have centred on production rather than reproduction.

Furthermore, researchers are likely to share the conventional definition of the 'political' derived as it was from the male-dominated public domain (Novarra 1980; Stacey 1980). They thus reproduce and reinforce the gender order and the associated mobilization of bias. The covert grievances of women are there-

7

fore less likely to be uncovered than those of men. Indeed, as Stephen Lukes has argued, the subordinate group itself, in our case women although he does not extend his argument to them, may be unaware of its 'real' interests and subscribe to the inevitability or desirability of the *status quo*. Lukes (1974) argues that while decisions are choices consciously or intentionally made between alternatives, the bias of the system can be mobilized, recreated, and reinforced in ways that are neither conscious nor intended. He argues that a dominant group may be so well entrenched that it is unaware of any potential challenge or of any alternatives (1974 : 21). For Lukes it is not simply a matter of individual decisions or actions, it is a matter of socially and culturally patterned behaviour exhibited by groups and expressed in institutionalized form. In this argument, actual or potential conflict is no longer a necessary criterion for the exercise of power. Wrong (1979) finds a problem with this argument in so far as what is under discussion is social control and not power relations. The power dimension is one aspect of the way in which a well-entrenched and normatively-supported system of social control is maintained. We take Wrong's point that in such a system power is undoubtedly exercised over those, notably the children, who have not yet internalized the values of the normative order. We would wish to argue, however, that power does not cease to be exercised when such values have been internalized.

It is not our intention to argue that there is some sort of conspiracy at work. Ideologies that legitimate action are promulgated and perpetuated much more subtly. Notions of the 'proper place' and 'proper behaviour' are deeply ingrained and emotionally loaded, such that acute discomfort is felt when the norms are violated. For to the actors concerned, the norms have come to appear as 'natural', as part of an externally given order without which there could only be chaos. Thus deviants must be put down and the order maintained. But most people do not think to deviate. And this is as true, of course, for those without power in a given order as it is for those with power.

This view is in line with that of Westergaard and Resler (1975), who argue in their analysis of power in capitalist society that there are those who have the passive enjoyment of advantage and privilege, supported by institutional practices, which are not challenged.

> 'In any society, the pattern of people's lives and their living conditions take the forms which they do, not so much because somebody somewhere makes a series of decisions to that effect; but in large part because certain social mechanisms, principles, assumptions . . . are taken for granted. . . . The favoured group enjoys effective power, even when its members take no active steps to exercise power. They do not need to do so – for much of the time at least – simply because things work their way in any case.' (1975 : 142–43)

Power for Westergaard and Resler inheres not just in individuals or groups but in anonymous social mechanisms and assumptions, in social institutions. In this way they argue that the continued power of capital is revealed not in individual acts of decision-making, but in the everyday application of 'those assumptions which give priority to private capital accumulation and market exchange in the use and distribution of resources' (1975 : 144).

One can approach the question of women in relation to public affairs from an analagous perspective, in terms of the assumptions and mechanisms that continue to define politics as the affairs of men. This approach can be no more than by analogy, for the Marxist as well as all other perspectives uses concepts derived from the public domain. In writing this book we have therefore found it necessary to develop our own theoretical approach, and for this we have drawn upon a number of schools of thought. We have rejected a behaviourist pluralist approach not only because it has defined politics in such a way that the great majority of women are left out, but also because its basis is individualistic and ignores the importance of social structures, social groups, and social control. The sociological debates on the nature of power contribute to our thinking (and see the recent retranslation of Weber (Walliman, Rosenbaum, Tatsis, and Zito 1980)) as does the Marxist understanding of the class structure and of class dynamics. Feminists have found it necessary to develop the concept of patriarchy to explain facets of the social structure and social process that are responsible for the continued subordina-

9

tion of women. We follow this argument in insisting that issues of women and politics can only be addressed if attention is paid to the familial institutions of societies. These institutions alone cannot explain the contemporary public political status of women. For this, reference must also be made to the class structure, to the state as a set of semi-autonomous institutions, and to the ways in which they relate to the familial order (cf. Mitchell 1971; Rowbotham 1974a; Eisenstein 1979).

Our approach is therefore in one sense catholic; in another sense we are attempting to develop a distinctive feminist theoretical position. This we attempt to test against empirical data gathered by scholars in a variety of traditions.

Men may from time to time act to maintain their power and authority in the gender order. This they only have to do when challenged by 'impudent lasses', but in general they have not had much need; the impudent are few in number. As Jean Baker Miller has it, 'Dominants prefer to avoid conflict – open conflict that might call into question the whole situation' (1976 : 9). It becomes clear that the question of women and power cannot be addressed from the public domain alone; it is a question of the relationship of that domain and the private domain of the family, between which, for many years, the men were the mediators.

In not thinking to deviate from the established order, women have been architects of the reproduction of their own oppression. Women in the family particularly participate in a system that upholds a division of labour that removes them from public life. In the roles they adopt in the family and their differential treatment of their own children of different sexes, they help to perpetuate gender roles that ensure a subservient role for women. So we argue in the pages that follow that the institution of the family and the ideologies which support it are useful for those presently holding power. For these reasons, it is surprising how far women have come in seeking to upend the social arrangements which have existed for millenia before.

It is also a question of the many and subtle ways in which dominance is exercised. Women are beginning to explore the ways in which we are led to adopt and uphold self-images and definitions of reality which conform to men's interests. Women are not only discovering that the 'personal' is, after all, 'political'

(Lipshitz 1978; Millett 1976) but are also searching for alternative social realities in which women have not always been the second sex. As we show in Chapter 2, while there may never have been a 'golden age' in which women held ultimate power, the idea of a matriarchy has provided an important alternative political vision as well as a stimulus for feminist research. In our case, it prompted us to explore the circumstances in which some women have exercised power, especially as these are related to the relationship between the private and public domains.

We seek to show that in Europe women shared power with men until the state was separated from the household, when it became a public domain of the men; how this division proceeded as the centralized state developed and was further exacerbated by the division of the workplace from the home as capitalist industry developed. We argue that adult female suffrage gave legal recognition to an utterly new status for women to act as individuals in their own right, rather than as members of families; but that women did not have an organized support basis upon which to translate this legal right into a social reality. We seek to show that the developments in capitalist formation and in the control exercised by the state, including paradoxically the legislation that has sought to liberate women (or at least give them equality of status), have had the effect of dissolving the hitherto existing distinction between the private and the public domains. What was once the private domain of women has been undermined and invaded by professionals and agents of the state, advising and guiding; in the guise of the 'egalitarian, democratic family' men have invaded, or been welcomed into, the kitchen, so that women no longer have a private territory to command nor belong to an organized group of female kin. At the same time they have been offered the trappings of a fair share in the public domain, but not the reality of equality and responsibility; their continued but not autonomous domestic role has precluded this.

As Rowbotham (1973) has argued, women continue to be invisible in the man's world (what we term the public domain) which they may enter so long as they behave there as men. She also makes plain the delicate and difficult nature of women's struggle for liberation, affecting as it does the most intimate facets of life, the enemy in the bed, of social relations with children as well as

11

mate. In this sense it is quite different from the workers' struggle for a share of the power. It is partly for these reasons that women, unlike working-class men, lacked power bases to go forward to seize advantage of their newly found legal rights. While the workers' struggle may involve the elimination of the enemy, that is, the very categories of capital and labour, women's liberation, will inevitably have to find a place for men in its new order.

Thus we argue in the pages that follow that women have a long way to go before they may be said to have achieved a fair share of public and private power. At the same time we remain astonished at what has been achieved in a short half-century.

TWO

The private domain of women: the family as a power base

'The view that women are inextricably bound together in subjection to a common and unchanging oppression is a patent oversimplification.' (Bujra 1978 : 28)

'The powerful position of Iroquois women was the result of their control of the economic organization of their tribe.' (Brown 1975 : 251)

What women have been trying to do in the last 200 years has been very radical. They have, for the first time in history, been trying to achieve some independence as persons and to exercise some power as individuals in their own right. Women have had power before, but always as members of families. In the modern period they have been struggling to share in the individualism which became the right of men as a concomitant to industrial capitalism. When people say that women have had the vote for fifty years and look what little use they have made of it, how little they have achieved, we reply that it is astonishing how far women have come in so short a time. This is especially so since the institution of the family has not undergone any radical change.

Was there a matriarchy?

Women have had political power in the past. When power derived from the family women shared in it. This was Engels's argument, derived from Morgan, in *The Origin of the Family* (1960). Indeed, there are those who argue that at one time women ruled in the family and from this position were the rulers of the whole society: that there was a matriarchy.

How good is the archaeological evidence that there were ancient matriarchies? Rosaldo and Lamphere (1974) conclude that the evidence from antiquity is hard to come by and not clear-cut.

Goddess–worship

Merlin Stone (1976) has argued that originally goddess-worship was supreme in a great part of the ancient world, later to be destroyed by the spread of Judeo-Christian religions. She argues also that goddess-worship may well have been associated with matrilineal societies, i.e. societies where descent is reckoned through the female line. It does not follow, of course, that matrilineal descent implies matriarchy. In known matrilineal societies it is often the brother of the mother who plays the dominant role, the role occupied in modern Western society by the husband-father. The mother's brother in such societies has responsibilities for the family, for the children, and on behalf of the family to other members of the society. However, Stone argues that the worship of goddesses is likely to have affected the status of women in a number of ways, and may also have reflected an asymmetry biased to women rather than to men. She argues that the goddesses were worshipped not only for their beauty, sexuality, and fertility, but that they were also thought to be the source of all knowledge, wisdom, law, and other characteristics, all of which were later thought to emanate only from

14

male gods (and from men). She quotes Jacquetta Hawkes (1958) who, talking about goddess-worship in Crete, suggests that the goddess may have been a male dream but 'Cretan men and women were everywhere accustomed to seeing a splendid goddess queening it over a small and suppliant male god, and this concept must surely have expressed some attitude present in the society that accepted it.' (Stone 1976 : 65). The gender order suggested is clearly different from that of many Christian religions where the Church is dominated by the male figure of Christ while Mary the Mother of God is represented in a side aisle or chapel, occupying a nurturant role cradling the infant king.

Catholicism and Marianism

The *consciousness* of what it is to be a man or a woman is obviously portrayed differently in these religions. Women and men in goddess societies had the symbolism of dominant and powerful female figures constantly held up before them. One would expect that this might have affected women's vision of what it was possible for them to do, just as one might have expected that the inferior and nurturant role allocated to Mary the Mother of God might have similarly limited women's vision to domestic and subservient roles. It does seem that in Catholic countries women have been confined to a sphere in which their greatest contribution, unless they remain celibate and thus pure (Ruether 1974 : 150–83), is the production and rearing of children and the service of men. In practice, however, this has not necessarily left them without some power and influence within that domain and also derived from it. The cult of Marianism (Stevens 1973), a movement within the Roman Catholic church, has as its object the special veneration of the figure of the Virgin Mary. Stevens argues that while in the early Christian church the Jewish patriarchal notions were dominant, by 431 AD the female figure had entered Christian dogma, probably deriving from the Mediterranean goddess religions. From there the cult of Marianism was later taken to Latin America where it was reinforced by Amerindian mother-god worship.

Subsequently Latin American secular society has become distinguished by an excessive veneration of women, greater according to Stevens than that found in Europe where Marianism has flourished, and different also in quality. *Marianismo*, the counterpart to the male *machismo*, has developed. This involves a notion of women as having semi-divinity, moral superiority over men, and spiritual strength. At the same time they are infinitely submissive to their men whom they serve unceasingly. The women are essentially sad, the classic *mater dolorosa*, because of the sinfulness of the men which will consign them to an after-life of purgatory. Stevens argues that although at first glance the women appear to be subjected to a tyrannical male rule, they have strong influence over male children in the household.

It appears that women in the mestizo society of which Stevens writes accept and are comfortable with their privatized but venerated position. Whether this is a question of their failure to perceive the inferiority of their position and therefore their lack of consciousness of their oppression, or whether their real interests (see Lukes 1974 : 24–5) are served by their present status, Stevens does not discuss, nor does she offer the evidence to make a judgement possible. What is clear is that the venerated position of these women is deeply embedded in the family and kin and is based entirely on the notion of the mother. In this sense here, as elsewhere, Marianism reinforced the familial role of women. It did not widen the range of what women saw it as possible for them to do.

Goddess–worship and woman–power

One might expect the goddess vision to be associated with a greater equality in practice between women and men than might be found in a society dominated by male gods. Stone (1976) gathers evidence which suggests that in most parts of the Near East in ancient times women at least had a freer and more equal position in relation to men than they did in Israel where the male Yahweh (Jehovah) was worshipped and women were formally subordinated to men. The traditional Jew still gives daily thanks that he was not born a woman. Stone reports the accounts of Diodorus Sicilus in North Africa and the Near East which include many statements reporting a high or even dominant status of women. Diodorus admires and respects women who wielded power and were warriors. She reports on Ethiopian women who carried arms, practised communal marriage, and raised their children communally, often themselves becoming confused as to who the mother had been. In Libya she says that all authority was vested in the woman, who discharged every kind of public duty, while the men looked after domestic affairs and did as they were told by their wives. In Egypt she also says wives had authority over their husbands.

On balance, the evidence that Stone produces encourages a view of the worship of females, of powerful priestesses who attended the goddesses, of women involved in trading and owning property which they passed to their children in their line. As Stone says, the arguments about female status and female deities have something of a chicken-and-egg quality: which came first?

Peggy Sandray (1974) inclines to the view that the belief system will be developed to legitimize the prevailing distribution of economic and political power and thus that the existence or development of female deities can be seen as a means for recognizing and accepting female power. She computed for twelve societies the percentage of deities who were female and the percentage of these who had clearly-defined general power over both males and females, and related this to the status of women in the public domain (economic and political) in those societies. She found a high correlation between the percentage of deities who are female and the contribution of females to subsistence, but no correlation between the percentage of female deities and female status in the public domain. However, she found a low but positive correlation between the percentage of female deities with general powers over both males and females and female status.

Matriarchies unlikely in past or present

It seems likely that matrilineality (property passing in the female line) may have been associated with goddess-worship and that in these societies women were not subordinated as wholly as they are in patriarchal, patrilineal, patrilocal societies. Whether women ever ruled supreme seems less likely. The evidence for a matriarchy is slender and dubious, as Paula Webster (1975) concluded after a careful survey. Rosaldo and Lamphere (1974) share

17

her view. Webster argues, however, that we need 'sharper, explicit and cross-culturally applicable definitions of power, authority, influence and status' (Webster 1975 : 154) and that we need, as well as visionary work that seeks to create new models of society, revisionary work that seeks to locate women's power *within* male-dominated societies. Arguments that assume total oppression are as inaccurate as those that assume a golden age of power. They may serve a useful ideological purpose in a struggling women's political movement. But they will not aid our understanding of the mechanisms whereby power is wielded, how it is distributed, and how that distribution might be made more equal. We have to make our vision of what equality of power might be like clearer, while at the same time analysing the empirical distribution of power historically and contemporarily.

The importance of power from the private domain

Cynthia Nelson (1973, 1974), asserting that private power should be examined alongside public power, has studied the extremely male-dominated nomadic tribal societies of the Middle East. There, women are commonly said to have no sense, to be like children in this and other ways, and to be irresponsible with money. Nelson shows that in these nomadic tribes ethnographers agree that there are two social worlds 'the tent and the camp – in which the former is the private domain of the woman, and the latter is the public domain of the man' (1973 : 44). But ethnographers disagree on the basic character of power and authority. Barth, a Western male ethnographer, sees the women as exercising considerable autonomy and authority in the domestic domain: 'the internal authority pattern of Basseri is similar to the urban Western family' (Nelson 1973 : 45, quoting Barth 1961 : 15–16), while a male Arabian ethnographer, Asad, claims that among the Kababish, men are responsible for all the domestic economics and family decisions, the men being dominant overall. Nelson suspects that this is the view of his *male* informants. She quotes (1973) similar views reported by Emanuel Marx (1967 : 186) for the Bedouin of the Negev, and by Emrys Peters (1966 : 1) for Cyrenaica but she (Nelson 1973 : 49) is able to quote a Marri woman from the work of Robert and Jean

18

Pehrson (1966 : 59) who, describing the highly segregated life of women and men, says 'What do they know about what their women do?'

Drawing on the work of Emrys Peters (1966), Ian Cunnison (1966), and of some female ethnographers such as Ilse Lichtenstädter (1935), Safia Mohsen (1970), and Mathea Gaudry (1929), Nelson concludes that women in practice have a good deal of power, including power over men. This view is confirmed by Constantinides (1978) writing of Muslim women in the North Province of Sudan who, she says, have considerable informal influence although they have no formal role in economic or political decision-making. Maher (1976), writing of Moroccan women, argues that although the public sphere, which includes all political, legal, and commercial transactions, is reserved for men, women can exercise power in that domain. The women she studied exercised this influence through the 'women's network' and through patron-client relations among women.

Nelson found that women could exercise power because they link men together through marriage. Marriage ties were of great significance and women were able to influence these arrangements for their children. Women were important in their own domain and, through their power in that domain, they could influence the public domain of the men. They controlled food, sex, and the supernatural. They could influence the political careers of men by making or breaking their reputations so that policy decisions taken by men in public had to take account of the reactions of the women. Although women lacked public power, as totally as any women anywhere, they were not powerless. But they remained profoundly inferior. As Cynthia Nelson concludes:

'From the ethnographic literature on nomadic societies there is ample evidence to support the idea that the woman defines herself and her position in terms of values centred about the man. She then uses the male-centred value-system to attain her own ends by way of manipulative techniques that force man to recognize female power without losing his self-esteem.' (1973 : 56)

Saifullah-Kahn (1976) comes to similar conclusions about the

Muslim women of Pakistan where there are two clearly-defined worlds. She argues that these worlds are exclusive and that the very existence of two exclusive worlds ensures their interdependence. This 'results in a far greater bargaining power for the women than is usually acknowledged' (Saifullah-Kahn 1976 : 234). In the Shi'a sect, a minority in most Islamic countries but a majority in Bahrein and Iran, women attend the Mat'am (place of crying), a centre for festivals and the religious education of women. The women go to the Mat'am to mourn the death of Hussein (over 1,000 years ago) and to weep for the transgressions of their sons, over whom they thus exercise considerable control (cf the *mater dolorosa* of Marianism). In Muhurran, in the procession where men flagellate themselves, which is also associated with the death of Hussein, the men walk in groups according to their women's Mat'am. Women preachers of the Shi'a sect from time to time have their air fares paid to preach in Iraq and in other parts of Islam. In Bahrein and Iran, as elsewhere in Islam, women are in general defined by their relationships to men, but in the Shi'a sect they not only act independently but also in the religious world, part of the public domain normally exclusive to men. The women are thus organized separately from their families and beyond the limits of the private domain. Their organization includes a potential for international action (Stacey and Stacey 1979).

Sandray's (1974) cross-cultural contemporary evidence suggests that there is a wide range of variation in female public status. In a few of the cases she discusses she found evidence that both women and men have power and authority in the public domain, although in the majority of cases men clearly had higher public status (1974 : 205).

The Iroquois women are among the few where considerable power is exercised in the public domain, the women having power to nominate Council Elders and to influence Council decisions. Brown's (1975) view is that this power derived from the control that women had over the economic organization of the tribe. But still this power derived from a familial position. The women with the power were the *matrons*.

The exclusion of women from the public domain because of their power

In the Western world the explanation most often given for the exclusion of women from the public domain rests upon the inferiority of the female sex. Fatima Mernissi (1975) argues that the segregation and oppression of women in Islam arises not from this thesis but from the assumption that woman is a powerful and dangerous being. Her danger lies particularly in her sexuality. Mernissi argues that 'in societies where seclusion and surveillance of women prevail, the implicit concept of female sexuality is an active concept; in societies where there are no such methods of surveillance and coercion of the woman's behaviour, the concept of female sexuality is a passive concept' (1975 : 3). Mernissi refers to the Muslim feminist, Kacem Amin, who concluded that sexual segregation is a device to protect *men*, not women, because women are better able to control their sexual impulses than men. What is feared is *fitna*, disorder or chaos (*fattan*, from the same root, also means beautiful woman). 'Social order is secured when the woman limits herself to her husband and does not create *fitna* or chaos by enticing other men to illicit intercourse (*zina*)' (1975 : 10). *Fitna* may occur whenever a man is faced with a woman. Hence the social world is strictly divided into two spaces, the male and the female, women being refused access to the male world and having to conform to various symbols of separation such as the veil. This seems similar to, but different from the Hindus of Northern India for whom Sharma (1978) reports 'a widespread belief that female sexuality is more difficult to control than that of man' (Caplan and Bujra 1978 : 280).

In contrasting the women of Islam with the women of the West, Mernissi has largely relied on published sources, a fair comparison with the writings of the prophet. Among the common people in Britain belief in 'powers' lingered into the nineteenth and twentieth centuries, many years after the élites had ceased to believe, and no longer tried witches. Thus if a woman crossed the path of a miner in the Northern coalmining town of Ashton (Dennis, Henriques, and Slaughter 1974) on his way to the pit, he would not go down, for she would have

21

certainly brought him ill luck. We do not know what accomoda tions the men made when the women worked underground; the were not then 'taboo' as they now are. Seabrook (1973 : 38 reports for Northamptonshire earlier this century how distresse the folk in the boot and shoe manufacturing villages were whe the labour shortages of the Second World War led to the employ ment of women in the local butchers'. This was frightenin because one had no means of knowing whether the women serv ing were 'like that' (menstruating) which would certainly pol lute the meat. It may be that Mernissi (1975) has underestimate the Western man's fear of the supernatural power of womer Certainly many years after *Coal is our Life* (Dennis, Henrique and Slaughter 1974) was written one of us women was take down a mine (not in Yorkshire) by the miner's agent. In the firs place a woman could not go down or anywhere undergroun unless another woman was with her throughout. When th author finally reached the coal face she was taught the loca men's swearwords (as if she did not know them already, a know ledge which she certainly did not admit to them). The interpreta tion would be that she was being made an 'honorary male' for th purpose of the visit to obviate the disorder that the presence of woman at the coal face implied: the threat of chaos, of disruptio of the order. Thus do superstitions continue to support the con temporary gender order.

It may therefore be that part of the suppression of women in th West has derived from their potential danger in somewhat th same way as the Muslim women Mernissi describes. Perhaps th definition of women as weak covers male fears as deep-seated a those of Islamic men who define women as powerful but inferior It could also be that the fear of the women's powers is not wha leads to their oppression, as Mernissi implies, but that havin oppressed women, men are fearful of their restlessness, thei possible uprising, or, more dangerous because invisible, the exer cise of their supernatural powers against men.

The segregation of domains associated with nascent capitalism

The Islamic social order was imposed by the Prophet Muhammed Accounts suggest that before Islam women were self-determinin

22

and could choose and discard their sexual partners at will. The physical father was considered unimportant and there was no question of paternal legitimacy. This female self-determination was possible because a woman was backed by her own people.

Women, and royal women are particularly mentioned, resisted the coming of Islam.

> 'The revolutionary new structure of Islam was based on male dominance. Polygamy, repudiation, the prohibition of *zina* and the guarantees of physical paternity were all designed to foster the transition from family based on female self-determination to a family based on male control. The Prophet saw the establishment of the male-dominated Muslim family as crucial to the establishment of Islam.' (Mernissi 1975 : 28)

The communal tribal society was breaking up when the Prophet was preaching. Women less often had their own people to back them.

Mernissi describes graphically the fear of chaos, of disruption of the social order that Muslims feel women might cause if they are not subjugated and subordinated. She does not analyse why this is so feared. She does, however, describe how the tribal society was breaking up in the face of the development of a mercantile economy with an accompanying move from communalism to individualistic pursuits. It would appear that concepts of property were being enhanced and that many of the rules established by the Prophet were to ensure the consolidation of property in the hands of men through the family system. Under the old tribal communalism women had no institutionalized access to property through inheritance which was the privilege of those who took part in battles and acquired booty, i.e. able-bodied males (Mernissi 1975 : 38). One might compare this suggestion with similar conclusions reached by Bujra (1978 : 22–5, 31–4) who discusses relationships between the mode of production and sexual division of labour in pre-capitalist societies.

Mernissi describes 'the genius of Islam' in connecting communal and self-serving tendencies together:

> 'The communal tendencies were channelled into welfare for the Pax Islamic and the self-serving tendencies were mainly given release in the institution of the family which allowed

23

> new allegiances, *new ways to transfer private possession of goods*, while providing at the same time tight controls over women's sexual freedom.' (Mernissi 1975 : 39, our emphasis)

Under the pre-Islamic arrangements paternity was never clear; property passed in the matriliny from a man to his sister's son. Islam established the concept of fatherhood and legitimacy within the family thus allowing 'full expression to the believer's self interest' (Mernissi 1975 : 39). The *idda*, whereby it is forbidden to a widowed or divorced women to have sexual intercourse until several menstrual cycles have passed, was instituted to ensure paternity.

Women not powerless but divided

The division of the social worlds into male and female leaves the male with power in the public and religious world as well as in possession of the property. But as in the nomadic tribes there is some power in the hands of the women. The mother-in-law relationship is particularly strong, the mother having rights in the choice of her son's wife and also restraining the closeness of the relationship between a man and his wife by her continual presence. While power and authority are hierarchically organized in favour of men the division of power and authority in the household divides the women. A wife lives in her mother-in-law's household and is ritually and materially subservient to her. She not only must make symbolic obeisance, but is also dependent upon her mother-in-law for access to the food store and to the money of the household. This division among the women in their own domain is one which is constantly referred to in the work on women's solidarity edited by Caplan and Bujra (1978). So often the organizations of women, and the power they exercise, support and maintain male-dominated institutions or the associated class-divided societies.

The vision of woman–power

Mernissi argues that Islam fears woman-power and that there are two theories, explicit and implicit, about female sexuality: the

24

explicit theory argues that men are aggressive and women passive, while in the implicit theory civilization is struggling to contain women's destructive and all-absorbing power. The threat of this breaking out (*fitna*) is all-pervasive, and intensified in contemporary Morocco where women are increasingly invading male social space.

This fear of female power has something in common with some of the accounts of matriarchy. There are those who argue that the vision of the matriarchy is a male phantasy. Perhaps Diodorus' accounts were a sort of *Erewhon*, a kind of *News from Nowhere*, a vision, although both Herodotus and Sophocles also report women trading in the market place while their husbands stay at home and weave. Whether or not matriarchies were male phantasies, the vision of woman-power has importance.

Dan Lerner argued (1964) that for change to come about in a society, individuals have to achieve a vision beyond the confines of the traditionally-sanctioned ideology and behaviour of their society. Without this people would not make changes in their behaviour and thus produce change in the society. In the same vein Webster (1975) is right to argue that the vision of power that matriarchy offers is important to help women see beyond the frontiers of the male-dominated society in which most women now live. Michael Mann (1973) makes a similar point in relation to Western working-class movements: failure to have a clear enough vision of what a socialist society might be like has led to frequent defeats.

The modern women's liberation movement has looked for such models to use as symbols, to help raise the consciousness of women about their present oppression and to encourage faith in women's ability to achieve more than is normally expected of them in contemporary society. One model that offers an alternative to patriarchy is the myth of the Amazons, the society run by warrior women. However, after looking closely at the Amazon myth, Mandy Merck has warned the women's movement that it may not be a good model for them, because the myth was embedded in 'a culture distinguished . . . for its unusual degree of female subordination' (Merck 1978 : 96). Merck reminds us that myths are used for social, political, and economic ends. She traces the use made of the myth and the changes in it from the

25

early days of Ancient Greece through the times of Heracles and the age of black-figure art to the days of Theseus and the red-figure art. When Heracles was sent to do daring tasks he came back with the girdle of the Amazon Queen, but Theseus came back with the Queen herself. The red-figure art depicted Amazons as foreign, female, and erotically dominated by men; the painter focuses on the subordination of the Amazon, not just as foe, but as woman. The climax of this presentation is perhaps reached in the Parthenon, where the Amazons are clearly depicted as the female enemies of the state. Ultimately the Amazons are shown as anti-feminine, self-mutilating (cutting off their right breasts the better to fight), man-hating, and technically underdeveloped.

Thus the Amazon myth as used by ancient Greek politicians was one in which the women were seen as vanquished opponents of the state, defeated by the male heroes who had founded it in the mythical past. 'Patriotism reinforces patriarchalism to define the tribeswomen as opponents of the state . . .' (Merck 1978 : 96). Merck also suggests that the myth may have been used to legitimate female subordination, which was 'radical even by the standards of their Greek predecessors and contemporaries' (Merck 1978 : 108). The chief obligation of citizen women was to produce male heirs for war and for family continuity. There was conjugal sexual abstinence, female infanticide, male but not female homosexuality, and rigorous penalties for adultery. Women never came of age, were always minors at law, and under the guardianship of a man. They worked in the home along with the slaves on work which was defined as unfit for citizens.

Merck suggests that unease must necessarily have resulted from such inequality and that the Amazon myths were an expression of that unease, the fear of female rebellion. The myth eased the tension by representing that rebellion as already having taken place and having been satisfactorily concluded in the deserved defeat of the women. Bamberger (1974) (whom Merck quotes) comes to a similar conclusion with regard to the South American myths of warrior women, where female rule is seen as the catastrophic alternative to male domination. These myths reiterate that women did not know how to handle power when they were in possession of it and thus ' "reaffirms dogmatically the inferiority of their present position" ' (Merck 1978 : 108). Merck finally concludes that the Amazon myth cannot be taken over by the women's movement, for it is too deeply embedded in patriarchy, but that its consideration has been important because it is related to 'our genuine identification with women in struggle – a new will to power born of the unease of our own patriarchal era' (Merck 1978 : 113).

Shared domain: shared power

Whether matriarchy in antiquity was historical fact, vision, or phantasy, what is clear is that throughout all the known world and in history, wherever public power has been separated from private power, women have been excluded. But private and public power have not always been separate. Rosaldo and Lamphere (1974 : 1–16) show that where men and women share in the same domain all kinds of power and authority tend to be shared more equally. Certainly this is the lesson of European history – before the public domain was separated from the private, women exercised power.

Power from the family

This point is nicely discussed for the sixth to twelfth centuries in Europe by McNamara and Wemple (1974). In Rome there was an early and clear concept of public power and women were expressly excluded from it. At the same time Roman women could exercise considerable power, despite their privatization, if they accumulated property which they were able to do. In Carolingian times private power was hardly distinguished from public power, and there were therefore few restrictions on the power of women in any sphere of activity. 'Carolingian queens were housewives. But the houses they kept were the imperial domain itself' (McNamara and Wemple 1974 : 109). In the first feudal age, as the empire of Charlemagne was breaking up, the family was very important and the key to power was the control of landed property through private ownership or the control of royal property received as a fief. Daughters as well as sons shared in the property and the fiefs and some women were in this way able to exercise considerable power. But by the twelfth century public power was gradually being recaptured from the great aristocratic families by kings and princes. Institutions outside the family were being created to administer public affairs. As impersonal machinery for government was developed the women were excluded. 'With the return of public power and the corresponding loss of family power, women were moving back to the conditions that had existed under the Roman Empire' (McNamara and Wemple 1974 : 115).

THREE

The separation of the family from public power

'It has been suggested that the earlier English Commonwealth did actually embrace both men and women in its idea of the "Whole", because it was composed of self-contained families consisting of men, women and children, all three of which are essential for the continuance of human society; but the mechanical State which replaced it, and whose development has accompanied the extension of capitalism, has regarded the individual, not the family, as its unit, and in England this State began with the conception that it was concerned only with male individuals. Thus it came to pass that every womanly function was considered as the private interest of husbands and fathers, bearing no relation to the life of the State, and therefore demanding from the community as a whole no special care or provision.' (Clark 1919 : 307–08)

Medieval Women

Writing about medieval women, Eileen Power (1975) does not find it necessary to discuss women in politics at all, because there was no place for women in politics in the medieval order. She does show, however, that women were by no means without power in the familial, economic, and religious spheres.

Medieval ideas about women

> 'were formed on the one hand by the clerkly order, usually celibate, and on the other by a narrow caste, who could afford to regard women as an ornamental asset, while strictly subordinating them to the interests of its primary asset, the land. . . . Indeed it might with truth be said that the accepted theory about the nature and sphere of women was the work of the classes least familiar with the great mass of womankind.'
> (Power 1975 : 9)

Women were seen at one and the same time as the instrument of the Devil and the Mother of God. The first view was reinforced in secular life by the rhymed stories (*fabliaux*) which were brutally anti-feminist in their portrayal of women, and the second by courtly ideas of chivalry in which the woman was seen as superior in love. Nevertheless, women were placed in subjection to men, essentially through the institution of marriage, where obedience of a wife to her husband was exacted and where canon law specifically allowed wife-beating.

Few women revolted against this status. Christine de Pisan, at the end of the fourteenth century, championed women in her writings. She supported herself and her young children with her writing after she was widowed. Women also wrote pro-feminist poems and played a prominent part in heretical or near-heretical movements. In everyday life, furthermore, the subordination was imperfectly maintained. Women worked alongside men in the fields, traded in their own right in the towns, and helped to manage estates and lands.

Aristocratic women wielded great practical authority. The sphere of the home was theirs and they managed large households and perhaps also the home farm. An aristocratic lady, furthermore, was her husband's representative during his absence. The wives of prosperous burgesses also had a good deal of managerial responsibility and authority.

Such power and authority as those women wielded came from their position in the family and from the ownership of land and property. Nevertheless, their position did mean that some men, those of the labouring and servant classes, took orders from some women. Thus already in feudal times the subordination of women varied in kind from one level of society to another. Aristocratic and bourgeois women were able to wield some power, over men as well as other women, albeit derived from their marital or familial status.

Women also exerted power through the nunneries. The nuns, who were all of gentle birth, ran farms and sometimes large estates. Many men and women of the lower classes were dependent on them. They were under the control of the bishops, but were not always obedient to them (refusing, for example, to give up fashionable dress). The nuns, however, did not become priests, so although they wielded power and authority in the running of the nunneries and in the management of estates, they did not wield power within the Church or through the Church in the world.

McNamara and Wemple (1974) remind us how angry the Bishops at Nantes were in 895 at the political power that women at that period were able to exercise through their control of property, saying, ' "It is astounding that certain women, against both divine or human law, with bare-faced impudence . . . and with abandon exhibit a burning passion for public meeting, and they disrupt . . . the business of the Kingdom" ' (1974 : 112).

Power concludes, 'in the more exalted affairs of society, the military, the diplomatic, the political, the professional, women (save on exceptional occasions) influenced events comparatively little' (1975 : 53). Women only had public power in their own right in situations where there was no man to succeed. Thus did Elizabeth I come to the throne. Such inheritance was not possible in all royal families in Europe and marks off the English experience.

Among the labouring classes, in Power's view, there was a greater equality. The unmarried women of these classes worked to support themselves (as the gentlewomen went into nunneries)

31

and married women worked alongside their husbands or sometimes on their own account. Girls were apprenticed to women and to men to learn a trade. Sometimes women were members of guilds, but this seems to have been rare. Married women in trade were, in many towns, treated as single women. This was to protect their husbands who did not then have to cover them, but it did improve the status of married women under common law.

In the countryside women undertook the domestic work and child care and shared in all their husband's work. The widows and unmarried women had to do all these tasks on their own, and in addition were sometimes hired by the bailiff to do all sorts of agricultural labour. This was perhaps the most oppressed class of all. Not for them any power or authority. Peasant women who inherited property were in a somewhat different position: they owed labour although others may have performed the service for them (Middleton 1979 : 156).

The picture of women in medieval England is thus one in which women were formally subordinated to men by Church and State; in which they occupied no public positions of power; in which those of higher classes exercised power and authority in the woman's domain and on behalf of absent husbands over men as well as women; where women traded and had some economic independence; and where labouring women were subjected not only to men but to other women. Laslett (1971) confirms this general picture for as late as the mid-seventeenth century. He describes graphically how women were subsumed, along with servant men, unmarried men, boys and girls, into the personalities of their husbands, fathers, and masters. Mid-seventeenth-century England was in fact, according to Laslett, 'an association between the heads of . . . families, but an association largely confined to those who were literate, who had wealth and status, those . . . who belonged, with their families as part of them, to . . . the ruling minority' (Laslett 1971 : 20). 'To exercise power . . . to be free of the society of England . . . , you had to be a gentleman' (Laslett 1971 : 28). Assemblies other than of families occurred in battles, at the Assizes, the Quarter Sessions, the manorial courts, the town councils, the craftsmen's companies, the markets, the fairs, and the Parliament itself. In all of these assemblies women attended as well as men, although in all cases except for the markets they attended as spectators rather than participants. Their only public actions were as women of a family substituting for a man, most often for its head.

The transformation: seventeenth and eighteenth centuries

At the outset of the seventeenth century women still worked alongside men in the family and in domestic industry. Sometimes they engaged servants

> 'to free (themselves) from household drudgery. . . . No question arose as to the relative value of (the) work (of husband and wife), because the proceeds became the joint property of the family, instead of being divided between individuals.' (Clark 1968 : 294)

Alice Clark records how as the seventeenth century progressed the advance of capitalism and the development of the state diminished the value and worth of women as it diminished the value of the family and elevated the importance of the individual.

Some of the transformations that so affected the family and women by the end of the seventeeth century had had their roots in feudalism: the separate role of housewife had already emerged. (Middleton 1979 : 166). Other origins were in the early development of mercantilism. It was the agricultural revolution that affected the great mass of the people most profoundly and that led to the development of a class of free labourers (Marx 1973; Dobb 1947). This began a process through which some were able to accumulate capital by amassing land holdings, while others, landless, became wage workers. Among the larger landowning class, as the husband became relieved of his feudal obligations, so his wife was relieved of many of the former functions and duties in which she had supported him. She increasingly became a lady of leisure as the noble ladies already were in the medieval period.

The transformation was gradual and affected different classes and different parts of the country unevenly. Pinchbeck (1977) describes how at the outset of the eighteenth century, the wife of a large farmer took an active share in the management of the household, itself no light undertaking when all food and most of

33

the clothing were provided at home. Additionally, she may have had charge of the dairy, poultry, garden, and orchard together with their associated financial dealings; there were probably also servants to be supervised living in the house. The acceleration of the changes in the methods and organization of agriculture towards the end of the century freed these wives from a good deal of daily toil. But in Pinchbeck's view the lives of the new generation of women on larger farms compared unfavourably with those of their predecessors since

> 'there was not the same incentive for the farmer's wife to develop the business ability which had been essential before, and this, from one point of view, together with the release from all responsibility, was a distinct loss. The market and the many-sided activities of the household had provided excellent opportunities for the development and exercise of practical skill and business acumen which had no counterpart in the leisured life now adopted. The training in financial affairs and the knowledge that the family income consisted of the joint earnings of the farmer and his wife not only added interest to women's lives, but also tended to a development of independence and initiative.' (Pinchbeck 1977 : 34–5)

And independence, as Marshall (1969) has pointed out, is a form of power. These changes aroused heated criticism among some contemporaries. Arthur Young deplored the 'foolish farmers' who allowed their wives and daughters to live lives of 'folly, foppery (and) expence' (Pinchbeck 1977 : 35). John Robey's satiric gibe gives amusing and revealing testimony to the changes which took place from the eighteenth to the nineteenth centuries.

1743	*1843*
Man, to the Plough	Man, Tally Ho
Wife, to the Cow	Miss, Piano
Girl, to the Yarn	Wife, Silk and Satin
Boy, to the Barn	Boy, Greek and Latin
And your rent will be netted	And you'll be gazetted
	(Pinchbeck 1977 : 37)

For women whose husbands owned no land the problems were of a different order. 'Far from being excluded from production their life was one of ceaseless labour' (Rowbotham 1974b : 24). When there was no land, wives could not contribute to the resources of the family. 'If ultimately she became a wage earner, it was at a scale on which she could not adequately maintain herself, still less contribute to the support of the family' (Pinchbeck 1977 : 7).

The division of work and home

Although industrial women wage-earners were not unknown in the towns in the mid-eighteenth century, in the early stages of the industrial revolution some women were still able to work at home. Their domestic industry relied on merchants and entre-preneurs for raw materials and machinery; their labour contri-buted one part of the manufacturing process. Children and women worked together in the tasks of spinning and weaving. (Thompson 1963). However low the standard of living may have been, the family worked together as a productive unit. The increased concentration of manufacture in factories led to the development of a world of work that was separate from the world of the home, although at first it was not separate from the family as whole families were often employed together in factory labour. As Zaretsky puts it, 'work, in the form of wage labour, was removed from the centre of family life, to become the means by which family life was maintained' (1976 : 57).

The very tasks that working-class women were drawn into the factories to do produced the goods that relieved their more fortu-nate sisters of part of their housewifely tasks and rendered their skills redundant. At the same time as the economic power of middle-class men was thereby being strengthened, the power base of working-class husbands was being eroded through their wives' and their children's ability to earn money outside the home and outside the husband-father's supervision.

Engels was not the only contemporary commentator who felt that 'the social order makes family life almost impossible for the worker. . . . The husband works the whole day through, perhaps the wife also and the elder children, all in different places; they

35

meet night and morning only . . . what family life is possible under such conditions?' (Engels 1969 : 159).

But Engels was to realize later that the women's activity outside the home could form the basis of a new kind of union between a man and a woman, one which was not predicated on economic dependence. Marx shared this vision, saying:

> 'However terrible and disgusting the dissolution, under the capitalist system, of the old family ties may appear, nevertheless, modern industry, by assigning as it does an important part in the process of production, outside the domestic sphere to women, to young persons and to children of both sexes, creates a new economic foundation for a higher form of the family, and of the relation between the sexes.' (Marx 1954 : 460).

The bourgeoisie were anxious to restore and maintain order. Working men were anxious about their patriarchal authority and their employment. These twin anxieties combined to rob women of the potential equality which Engels had hoped waged work might bring them. Working-class men had an interest in restricting women's entry into the labour market or in limiting them to low-paid jobs. Their employers had a similar interest. In a situation where men were forced to compete with women, men's immediate short-term interests took precedence.

The workers themselves looked back to a 'golden age' when women and children worked in the home under the authority of husband and father. The idea of the patriarchal family persisted throughout the society at large, indeed was taking on a new and special form among the bourgeoisie as we shall shortly see. Many working men not surprisingly resented their loss of authority, fearing a threat to their masculinity. In this context the belief gained ground that a man's wage should be sufficient for his whole family, that women should not go out to work. The factory system was attacked for breaking up home production, for disrupting the rhythm of home and work, and for substituting the overseer's authority for that of the husband and father. Early unions began jealously to guard the primary right to work for the man with a family and kept an eye on employers who recruited women at reduced rates.

State intervention led to a succession of factory acts which

36

sought to control the hours and conditions of work of children and women. These measures on the one hand reduced some of the excesses of capitalist exploitation, notably of the mothers of young children. At the same time they had the effect of thrusting some women back into the home or into the ranks of a marginal or reserve labour force, a situation in which many found it very difficult to learn how to improve their lot. Many women, especially unsupported women, who had gained some small measure of independence began to feel that their livelihoods were in danger of being reformed away. The dual demands made upon women to help as needed in industrial production and to reproduce and to nurture the young imposed a heavy double burden. The contradictions of these demands were born by the women themselves. They did not lead to any fundamental change in the social order or to widespread state help. And the double burden increased their powerlessness.

> 'Reproduction, the long periods spent in child-bearing which interrupted the work routine, and female orientation within the family combined with middle-class propaganda about thrift, patience and individual self-help, to deflect the proletarianization of the working-class woman. The particular relationship of the women to reproduction and consumption within the family mediated her relationship to commodity production. . . . Women retained certain features of a pre-capitalist labour force. They never learned fully the rules of the new economic game. The corollary of this was a readiness to accept low pay.' (Rowbotham, 1974a : 113)

The attempt to impose bourgeois standards upon the working classes was another part of the middle-class effort to save the family and to preserve the social order. In this way, the early social workers emerged (see Wilson 1977 : 29).

The new family ideology

The family increasingly came to be seen as a refuge from a harsh world in which men were pitted against each other in merciless competition. As Ruskin put it, the home

37

> 'is the place of peace; the shelter, not only from all injury, but
> from all terror, doubt and division. . . . So far as the anxieties
> of the outer life penetrate into it . . . it ceases to be a home; it
> is then only a part of the outer world which you have roofed
> over and lighted fire in.' (Ruskin 1902, quoted in Zaretsky
> 1976 : 51)

In this ideology, women were to complete, sweeten, and embell-
ish the existence of others, and were idealized by virtue of their
confinement within the family. At the same time the number of
idle and ornamental wives increased. The fact that men and
women inhabited different spheres was reflected in assertions as
to their different capacities and natures: men were 'naturally'
aggressive, competitive, and protective; women were passive,
nurturant, and in need of protection. Treated like hot-house
plants, women were asked to aspire to being Angels in the House;
their helplessness, frivolity, and illogicality became part of the
commonsense knowledge of the day and a benign paternalism
began to mask their real powerlessness; it was the task of men to
protect such weak creatures from the outside world. Each sex was
thought to monopolize the characteristics consistent with its
proper sphere: for women the private, for men the public.

It was against a background such as this that Max Weber
analysed the rise of bureaucracy in terms of the divorce of the
office from the home and the end of the rule of notables. The
modern state was marked by the transition from a system based
on the influence of kinship and associated local groups to a
system which promoted 'the monopolization and regulation of
all "legitimate" coercive power by *one* universalist coercive
institution' (Weber 1978 : 337, emphasis in original). The consequent depersonalization of administrative management by
bureaucracy and rationalization of law completed 'the separation of the public and private sphere fully and in principle'
(Weber 1978 : 998).

The rise of public administration leaves the women at home

For Weber, just as the wage worker was separated from the means
of production as a result of the transition from feudalism to

38

capitalism so, by a parallel development, the civil servant was separated from the means of administration. Weber makes it clear that the development of the rational legal society involves the supercession of traditional or charismatic authority. 'Submission under legal authority is based upon an *impersonal* bond to the generally defined and functional "duty of office".' (Gerth and Mills 1948 : 299, emphasis in original.) It is characteristic of this society and of bureaucratic organization within it that persons subject to these commands are legal equals who obey the law rather than the person implementing it. 'It does not establish a relationship to a *person*, like the vassal's or the disciple's faith in feudal or in patrimonial relations of authority.' (Gerth and Mills 1948 : 199, emphasis in original.)

Although in practical politics and in his married life Weber was remarkably pro-feminist for one of his era (see Marianne Weber 1975 : 203, 371, 429) and certainly so in comparison with Marx, he did not extend this concern to his sociological analyses. He failed to note that women, despite the rise of citizenship, the establishment of equality before the law for all men, and the development of rational-legal authority, were still bound by traditional ties of loyalty and allegiance which he saw as inappropriate for the modern state. Mass democracy may have made 'a clean sweep of the feudal, patrimonial, and . . . plutocratic privileges in administration' (Weber 1978 : 984) for the men. It certainly did not do so for the women. For them until well into the twentieth century, as one of us wrote over twenty years ago, it is right that a housewife should return her occupation as 'married woman', for she cannot change her job without leaving her husband and children, nor leave her husband without losing her job. 'This is a unique status in a society otherwise based on individual contract, specialization, and separation of function' (Stacey 1960 : 136). In the nineteenth century women were not citizens. They were not even persons.

Furthermore the new administrative and political developments had the effect of reducing such power and influence as women had. The further the office, the party, and the seats of government were removed from the home, the less were women able to exercise influence upon the male public world through their fathers, husbands, brothers, sons, or lovers as they had

39

formerly done. The 'avocational administration by notables' (Weber 1978 : 984) was being superseded not only in administration but also in the political parties, particularly as the democratic mass parties developed. They were becoming bureaucratically organized under the leadership of party officials, professional party and trade union secretaries. The caucus democracy of Gladstone–Chamberlain in the 1870s was an early example of the supersession of notable rule based on personal relations and esteem.

Private influence or public action?

Nevertheless women continued to influence government from behind the scenes. As Ray Strachey points out, beautiful, clever, or ambitious women have used their personal charms and influence in all periods of the world's history 'and this fact was long considered a proof that the female sex had all the rights and power it could require' (Strachey 1978 : 33).

Caroline Norton, discussed in the next chapter, successfully used these methods to change family law in the nineteenth century. So long as women limited their attempts to influence government to this traditional method, it appears to have been acceptable or at least accepted. It was those women who came out in open political action who excited comment. A contemporary commentator on the canvassing activities of the Duchess of Devonshire and her sister in support of Fox in the late eighteenth century says 'they quite forgot their dignity, their womanhood, and Party was their watchword' (quoted in Iremonger 1961 : 215). When the world's Anti-Slavery Convention assembled in London in the 1840s the American delegation of seven included four women in contrast to the all-male British delegation. Amid much embarrassment and to the disgust of the American, William Lloyd Garrison, who arrived later and who was one of the most distinguished delegates, the women were put in a curtained gallery and forbidden to speak during the proceedings. Garrison declared he would share their exclusion and that he did (Fawcett 1912 : 13–14). The leading British representatives said that the claim that women should be part of the Convention was ' "subversive of the principles and traditions of the country, and contrary to the word of God" ' (Strachey 1978 : 41–2).

Nor were working-class women inhibited from taking political action. There was that 'monstrous regiment' of women who petitioned Parliament in the sixteenth century. Isolated working-class women spoke out from time to time, sometimes, as in the case of Joanna Southcott, associated with a religious message (Taylor 1978).

At the outset of the nineteenth century, working-class women were still taking political action. Dorothy Thompson (1976) has shown that working-class women were active participants in the politics of working-class communities until they apparently retreated into the home some time around, or a little before, the middle of the nineteenth century. Working-class women participated in the food riots and other demonstrations in the eighteenth and early nineteenth centuries. More than one account suggests that in these and in the later Chartist demonstration the women were in the forefront and more ferocious than the men. Women were on the councils of the reformers after the Napoleonic Wars, there were women's political unions and friendly societies and in some trades women were in unions. Women played an important part in the anti-Poor Law demonstrations of 1837 and throughout the Chartist movement from 1838 to 1848. Thompson quotes the Reverend Francis Close of Cheltenham who in 1839 complained that not content with using ' "their influence over their husbands, their brothers and their fathers to foment discord, to promote a spirit of sedition" ' they

> ' "now become politicians, they leave the distaff and the spindle to listen to the teachers of sedition; they forsake their fireside and home duties for political meetings . . . they become themselves political agitators – female dictators – female mobs – female Chartists!" ' (1976 : 127)

Thompson also records one of the rare cases when working-class women demanded the vote, in 1838 in Scotland, but she shows that their demands were usually more general than this. She also shows how ambiguous the Chartist movement was towards women, giving them a secondary role on the whole.

41

'Chartists of both sexes saw the main issue as one of class. The attainment of political power by the men of the working class would bring great benefits to the whole class, and the extension of political rights, on grounds of natural justice, to women might well be expected to follow.' (1976 : 132)

What is plain from Thompson's account is that women were often seen as participating in working-class politics as wives or sweethearts of the men, although this cannot have been the case in the all-women unions, friendly societies, and political groups. Thus Thompson quotes Banford as saying of his contingent in the march to St Petersfield on 16 August 1819: ' "At our head a hundred or two women, mostly young wives, and mine own amongst them. A hundred or two of our handsomest girls – sweethearts to the lads who were with us – danced to the music or sang snatches of popular songs" ' (1976 : 116).

There was a gender order too. Thompson quotes Henry Vincent, writing from Huddersfield in 1837 about a meeting called to form a working men's (sic) association, that the meeting took place in a hollow ' "the men all stood in the hollow, whilst the pretty lasses and women with white aprons and caps trimmed with green [the colour of protest], sat all around the sides of the hill" ' (1976 : 124).

Thompson speaks much, too, of radical *families*. The Lingars, where 'both sexes and more than one generation took part in local leadership' (1976 : 118) in Barnsley; Wilson of Halifax who learned his radicalism from his aunt; the Hansons of Elland in Yorkshire. The family connection, as well as the half-hearted feminism of the Chartists comes out, too, in the case of William Lovett who 'was happy to allow his wife to take over his position, *at half his salary*, when the First London Cooperative Trading Association could no longer afford to pay him to be storekeeper' (1976 : 132, our emphasis).

Thompson tells us that in the later Chartist period women were little in evidence. She is not fully able to explain this. In part there was 'the increasing influence of the temperance movement over women' (1976 : 136). In the early years women had joined men in the pubs. There was also the withdrawal of women from work outside the home. These may have been influences but they are not explanations. The change in the style of working-class politics away from mass politics to a form with more sophisticated organizations (the movement we discussed earlier and which Weber analysed) and the local vote for numbers of skilled workers may have contributed. Thompson argues that the way of life of the unskilled workers and the women did not allow their participation in more structured political forms which required regular working times and incomes. In the last analysis, Thompson suggests that the reason must be that the working-class women themselves came to accept the appropriateness of staying at home and caring for their children, and that along with this they accepted 'an image of themselves which involved both home-centredness and inferiority' (1976 : 137). The ideology developed by the bourgeoisie had been successfully passed on to the working class – to some extent through the middle-class charitable ladies who set out in mid-century to do good to their less fortunate sisters.

The men, and perhaps the working-class women themselves, had always seen the women's part as one that derived from their position in the family. Now they shared in 'The Victorian sentimentalization of the home and the family, in which all important decisions were taken by its head, the father, and accepted with docility and obedience by the inferior members (which) became all-pervasive and affected all classes' (Thompson 1976 : 138).

Women had not made a significant case for their independence as individual women. They were mostly in the movement as relatives of men, or so they were seen. The women, therefore, had no weapons against the mid-century reaction that restated in a new form the role of women in the family. Many working-class women continued to work, often in hard and brutal conditions, leaving no time or energy for politics, although the extent of women's work varied from one part of the country to another. Certainly, most working-class women withdrew from public activity and accepted privatization, a development their men must have shared and encouraged. It was not until the 1880s that working-class women were once again to take independent political action. The match-girls' strike of 1888, albeit led by the middle-class Annie Besant, was the most striking demonstration

43

of women's union action (cf. Ramelson 1972 : 106–07). In the meantime, along with their middle-class sisters, they had been effectively removed from power and influence except in the narrow arena of the family, from which all matters of politics had now been removed to the public arena. It is not surprising in a century in which increases in citizenship for men were sought through the means of civil rights that the excluded women should seek to share in these advances. For these reasons, the nineteenth-century feminist movement took the form of a suffrage movement to claim these new rights for women, although for many women much more than the vote was involved (see Mitchell 1968; Ramelson 1972).

At the same time as the rise of industrial capitalism led to the increased privatization of women and their removal not only from power but from influence, the seeds of the challenge to that system of women's oppression and the seeds of its ultimate destruction were sown. The bourgeois family was based on the notion of individualism. This individualism applied to men and their families, within which children and women were non-persons. Women, however, were human beings and it was inevitable that they should claim the rights of individualism for themselves. Thus it was that the early feminist movement, despite the many strands that have gone into feminism over the years,* concentrated on political power in the form of the vote. Thus it was also that women overlooked the immensely conservative tendencies inherent in the structure of their society and particularly of the institution of the family within it. Women were seeking to enter the public domain of the men without recognizing the implications of the private domain for their goal. In the following chapter we turn to the relations between individualism and feminism, and later look at the nature of the private domain of women.

* Olive Banks has summed these up as being evangelicalism, the enlightenment, and socialism (Banks, forthcoming).

FOUR

Individualism and feminism: the family and capital

'Feminism arose in England in the seventeenth century as a conglomeration of precepts and a series of demands by women who saw themselves as a distinct sociological group and one that was completely excluded from the tenets and principles of the new society. The seventeenth-century feminists were mainly middle-class women who argued their case in explicit relation to the massive change in society that came about with the end of feudalism and the beginning of capitalism. As the new bourgeois man held the torch up against absolute tyranny and argued for freedom and equality, the new bourgeois woman wondered why she was being left out.'
(Mitchell 1976 : 387)

Introduction: citizenship, social class, and woman

Among the changes that had been taking place and from which

women were specifically excluded was the development of the notion of citizenship, which has been ably and interestingly analysed by T.H. Marshall. Marshall defined citizenship as 'a status bestowed on those who are full members of a community. All who possess the status are equal with respect to the rights and duties with which the status is endowed' (1963 : 87). The emergence of the concept of citizenship was an essential part of the emergence of capitalism from feudalism. Under feudalism there had been 'no uniform collection of rights and duties with which all men – noble and common, free and serf – were endowed by virtue of their membership of society' (1963 : 75).

Marshall divided citizenship into three parts, civil, political, and social. Civil citizenship was that part which was necessary for individual freedom 'liberty of the person, freedom of speech, thought, and faith, the right to own property and to conclude valid contracts, and the right to justice' (1963 : 74). None of these rights were available to all women in the nineteenth century.

The second of Marshall's facets of citizenship was the political: 'the right to participate in the exercise of political power, as a member of a body invested with political authority or as an elector of the members of such a body.' (1963 : 74). The separation of political power from the home had, as we have seen, deprived all women of any such right: lower-class women had never been included. Marshall's third element, the social, the right to welfare and economic and social security, while having its roots in the nineteenth century, did not emerge for anyone until the twentieth century and is not central to our present argument.

As we have seen, the notion of individualism, of the individual personality, was one which was alien to the feudal era. The feudal social formation was based upon hierarchically organized collectivities in which the whole and not the individual parts was what was understood: people were categories rather than individuals and as such were replaceable. The concept of individualism had to develop, and the first aspect of citizenship, civil rights, had to emerge before capitalism could develop fully: citizenship was indispensable to the development of a competitive market economy. It gave to each man, as part of his individual status, the right to engage as an independent unit in the economic struggle.

Freedom to work was essential for the development of capitalism: serfs and bonded labourers had to be free to sell their labour; landlords had to be free to acquire land without the old customary entitlements. In the name of the liberty of the subjects the restriction of certain occupations to categories of people defined by their birthright was abolished. Feudalism as a total social, economic, and political system was dismantled, and capitalism emerged to replace it. What capitalism did was to replace one kind of inequality by another: the inequalities of the feudal system were incompatible with civil rights and individualism. But equality before the law did not imply social or economic equality. In place of feudalism rose the class system, or as Marshall has it civil citizenship provided 'the foundation of equality on which the structure of inequality could be built' (1963 : 91). We discussed some aspects of this new class system and its implications for women in the previous chapter.

While civil rights provided the basis for the emergence of capitalism, the rising bourgeoisie found that they also needed access to political power to defend and enhance their newly found economic position. The development of political rights in the nineteenth century was based on the claims of the new owners of property for recognition, a recognition that they, as much as the aristocrats, had a right to a say in government. New forms of government, more appropriate to capitalism, were beginning to evolve. We discussed the separation of administration from the home in the previous chapter. Following the successful attempts of the bourgeoisie, the 'men of property', to gain a share in government, men of the working class made similar demands: with each successive reform act in the nineteenth century increasing numbers of men were accorded political citizenship. In the nineteenth century political rights were treated as secondary to civil rights, civil rights gave the freedom to own property; property accorded the right to be involved in government. This position, as Marshall (1963) points out, was abandoned in the twentieth century when political rights were attached directly to citizenship. But in all of this only the men were involved, although certain *feme sole* who were property owners had

47

gained some limited rights to participation in local government in the nineteenth century. As Marshall points out, the vital change of principle involved in attaching political rights directly to citizenship 'was put into effect when the Act of 1918, by adopting manhood suffrage, shifted the basis of political rights from economic substance to personal status' (1963 : 81).

Marshall then goes on to point out that he did not mean 'manhood' in the generic sense implying all human beings: 'I say "manhood" deliberately in order to emphasize the great signifi- cance of *this* reform quite apart from the second, and no less important, reform introduced at the same time – namely the enfranchisement of women' (1963 : 81, our emphasis).

By inference the enfranchisement of women was for Marshall writing as late as the 1950s, something quite different from the emergence of political citizenship for men. That had been impor- tant because it was associated with the rise of capitalism women's freedom had not been necessary for that development We have not yet come across an analysis by Marshall of the 'no less important' enfranchisement of women, why it was initially denied and why later granted.

The analysis, as we attempt to show, has to be an altogether different one. In fact the historical order of the emancipation of women is different from that which was followed in the case of men, a point that Marshall fails to note. Women were in the end accorded political citizenship before they were granted full civil citizenship. Right until today there are certain civil rights that are not automatically accorded to married women. Feudal rela- tionships may have been dismantled for men, but they remained for women for years after. The status of women in the family was ascribed rather than being achieved as is an official position by the conclusion of entrance examinations or by election in the case of a parliamentarian. The status of women was ascribed in a way very similar to the ascription of status in the feudal era. This was particularly true of married women and it is here that the remnants of that status linger even today. (See Stacey 1960 discussed on p.39 above). Single women and widows always had something of a different status from their married sisters. They nowadays all have full civil citizenship. While ideas of citizen- ship associated with notions of individualism and equality

48

developed along with the rise of capitalism, women continued to be subsumed under the male head of household in what was quite a medieval manner. Women were not 'full members of the community' (Marshall 1963 : 87).

Women, freedom, and equality

Juliet Mitchell, in the quotation at the head of this chapter, locates the rise of feminism as a self-conscious movement of protest among bourgeois women in the specific circumstances in which citizenship and capitalism were developing. The rise of feminism in the seventeenth century was closely associated with the bourgeois notions about the equality of all mankind as the highest human goal. But the demands for liberty and equality were made on behalf of men only. Not surprisingly, there were, from an early period, women who resented their exclusion. Mitchell quotes Mary Astell as one example. Writing in 1700 Astell asked, ' "If *all Men are born free*, how is it that all Women are born slaves?" ' (Mitchell 1976 : 387, emphasis in original). It was the growth of early capitalism, of puritanism, and of new ideas of reason and science that provided the new perspective from which the 'insolence' of the 'impudent lasses' could draw strength and justification (Rowbotham 1974a : Chapter 1). 'Having got rid of the priest and proclaimed the priesthood of all believers, why confine divine inspiration to men?' (Rowbotham 1974 : 23).

What we propose to do in this chapter is to show how, from these beginnings and despite the many strands in feminism, the notion of individualism came to dominate the women's movement: demands were made to amend the marriage laws and accord domestic freedom to women; by the middle of the nineteenth century, individualism had led to increasingly successful demands that the public world, hitherto reserved for men, should be opened to women. Associated with these attempts, demands gradually concentrated on the attainment of women's suffrage as the most important goal on the road to achieving individual freedom and equality for women. In the same period in which women were being formally excluded from the public domain, they began to make their strongest claims to enter it:

49

indeed, that is partly why the formal exclusions (from voting, from entering the professions) took place. Articulate middle-class women were becoming an increasing threat to the male-dominated order. First, came a rising consciousness of women's unfreedom, then the struggle to loosen the bonds of marriage and the family and to enter the public world.

The rising consciousness of women's unfreedom

Mary Wollstonecraft at the end of the eighteenth century expressed her consciousness of women's unfreedom. On their behalf she joined in debate with Jean Jacques Rousseau, the great philosopher of the enlightenment. She argued in her *Vindication of the Rights of Women* (1792) against women's exclusion from the promises of political participation implied by the French Revolution and from hopes engendered by the notion of the Universal Rights of Man. She argued also against the results of this exclusion on the personality and image of women. Above all, she deplored the artificiality of demands placed on women by the idea of 'Femininity', the conventional nature of which was obscured even to those philosophers like Rousseau who had most to say on the subject of the rights of man. Rousseau believed that the true nature of man could only develop in freedom but at the same time condemned women to subjection. Wollstonecraft argued that the 'feminine' qualities of weakness and vanity, with which women were supposedly endowed by nature, were not inherent but acquired; that is, women were a socially oppressed group.

> 'I have, probably, had an opportunity of observing more girls in their infancy than J.J. Rousseau. I can recollect my own feelings, and I have looked steadily around me. . . . I will venture to affirm, that a girl, whose spirits have not been dampened by inactivity, or innocence tainted by false shame, will always be a romp.' (Wollstonecraft 1975 : 129)

Time and again Wollstonecraft refers to the damage done to women's sense of themselves by artificially imposed demands, the need for its correction and for the reintegration of women within the universe of Reason: 'I wish to show that elegance is inferior to virtue, that the first object of laudable ambition is to obtain a character as a human being, regardless of the distinction of sex' (1975 : 82).

Stone, whose careful archival work is a mine of information, argues that pleas such as these made by feminists in the seventeenth and late eighteenth centuries are unlikely to have had much effect in changing the relations between the sexes. 'The causes of those changes must be sought elsewhere, and the fears engendered in men by these indignant women probably inhibited change rather than speeded it up' (Stone 1977 : 343).*

What Stone does not understand or discuss are the tensions created for women in a situation in which, as he argues, they are becoming increasingly subjected to their husbands, increasingly confined to the home, and above all, in which the doctrines of individualism were being stressed on all sides. Protestantism, while increasing notions of equality and individualism, had assisted in the increased confinement of women. The *cri de coeur* of Mary Benson after the death of her husband, an Archbishop, expresses the oppression well:

' "This ceasing of every stimulus, and this terrible inner sense that all my life, all these years, was derived from and in answer to distinct, never ceasing claims seems to kill me. There is nothing within, no power, no love, no desire, no initiative: he had it all and his life entirely dominated mine. Good Lord, *give me a personality* . . ." ' (Moore 1974 : 89, our emphasis)

The feminist movements were an upsurge of anger against the contradictions of an unjust society. Would docility or silence or sweet quiet reason have helped the women more? Lawrence Stone's comments tell us more about the men than the women.

Trying to liberate the married women

Not all early feminists had such a philosophical turn of mind as

---

* Stone feels the same about the 'imperious demands' of the twentieth-century women's liberation movement for 'full sexual fulfilment' which he believes has the 'paradoxical result of reducing men to impotence . . .' (1977 : 681).

51

Wollstonecraft. For many of the early feminists and other women who fought for their rights it was the contradictions of their own situations that drove them to action (Rowbotham 1974b : 49).

Married women especially lacked freedom. The property, earnings, liberty, children, and conscience of married women belonged to their husbands, as Blackstone (1765) makes plain: ' "By marriage, the husband and wife are one person in law. . . . Upon this principle . . . depends almost all the legal rights, duties and disabilities, that either of these acquire by the marriage" ' (quoted in Acworth 1965 : 132). In other words, 'My wife and I are one and I am he' (Strachey 1978 : 15), or again, 'By marriage, the husband and wife become one person – and that person was the husband' (Stone 1977 : 195).

Living under the protective custody of men, women did not exist in law as persons in their own right, but were deemed to be 'under coverture'. Their legal status reflected the wife's subordinate status within the family. On becoming engaged to be married a woman could not legally make any gift without the prior consent of her fiancé; on marriage, the husband took a life's interest in the wife's land. All her personal fortune – including even her wardrobe and jewellery – became his property. Anything she might inherit or be allowed to earn also became his. She could only make a will with his consent, and even so, he could withdraw that consent at any time up to probate.

It was virtually impossible for a woman to dissolve a marriage. A wife could not leave her husband or remove children from the home without his consent. A husband's right to the custody of his wife meant that he was legally entitled to seize his wife's person if she left him, and relatives who gave refuge to a runaway wife could be sued in court by the aggrieved husband. Since he was entitled to consortium and service of his wife, if she was enticed away he could sue the enticer for damages and obtain compensation for loss of society and help in the home. If she left him, he could refuse maintenance and still demand that any monies earned by her be paid to him. For example, Acworth reports that in 1818, one Mrs Glover was living apart from her husband and supporting her children by her own earnings. Her husband gave notice that her salary should be paid to him. In judgement it was held that the husband was undoubtedly entitled to his wife's earnings (Acworth 1965 : 129). Being a legal minor, a wife could own no property. When Millicent Fawcett, a prominent suffragist, had her purse stolen, the thief was charged with stealing a purse and monies, the property of her husband, Henry Fawcett (Ramelson 1972 : 48). Furthermore, a husband could will his property away from his wife, including property that had been hers before marriage. On his death she was entitled to live in the marital home for forty days, provided she did not marry in the interim.

At the same time, a man was morally rather than legally bound to maintain his wife and she could not sue for maintenance. Under the Vagrancy Act of 1842, if a man neglected to maintain his wife so that she became chargeable to the parish, he could be deemed an 'idle and disorderly person', punishable with one month's imprisonment. The Poor Law Amendment Act of 1868 gave overseers of the poor power to summon an offending husband before the Magistrates' Court and obtain an order against him towards the costs of relief. But only the parish guardian or overseers were able to sue. Wives were still not able to bring actions for maintenance on their own behalf. Eighteenth-century legal commentaries concluded that since a married woman had no goods or property, her husband was liable to make good any wrongdoing on her part; Blackstone (1753) gave this as one reason for permitting a husband to chastise or beat his wife: 'as he is to answer for her misbehaviour, the law thought it reasonable to entrust him with his power of restraining her by domestic chastisement, in the same moderation that a man is allowed to correct his apprentices or children' (quoted in Acworth 1965 : 132). In the nineteenth century, husbands were not severely punished for maltreating their wives by comparison with the sentences imposed for theft or assault in pursuance of a crime. The sentences were lighter even in cases where the wife had suffered permanent injury. It seems likely that the judge, magistrate, or jury member, all of whom were men, assumed that the accused husband had simply been somewhat over-enthusiastic in exercising his indisputable right to chastise an erring wife.

All these laws make it plain that women were unfree to the point that they were considered to be the property of their husbands, having initially been the property of their fathers. This conclusion is reinforced by the accounts, which continue until the nineteenth century, of husbands putting up their wives for sale in the markets, sometimes leading them there by halter. Stone (1977) considers this practice to have been a method of obtaining divorce. It would certainly appear to be clear testimony to women's unfreedom. In 1797 the *Times* acknowledged the existence of the practice and indicated that it was a sign of progress in civilization that the market price of women had risen at Smithfield. Sometimes local authorities were involved: one parish officer persuaded a husband to sell his wife so that the parish should be relieved of the expense of her stay in the workhouse. ' "The master of the workhouse . . . was directed to take the woman to Croydon market and there, on June 17th, 1815, she was sold to John Earl for the sum of one shilling which had been given to Earl for the purchase." ' The receipt stated simply: ' "Received of John Earl the sum of one shilling, in full, for my lawful wife, by me. Henry Cook" ' (quoted in Acworth, 1965 : 125–6 and see also the account in *The Mayor of Casterbridge* (Hardy 1974 : 40)).

Yet Stone (1977) considers that in this period closer emotional ties had developed between members of the family, which became characterized by what he calls 'affective individualism', when the family came to be organized around the principle of personal autonomy and bound together by strong affective ties. Greater autonomy was granted to the wife and children and the home became private. Stone does not appear to recognize the implications for women of these developments in terms of privatization. Nor does he recognize that in being based on individualism the family carried within itself the seeds of its own destruction, for the women in it were profoundly restricted as we have seen, and were permitted little individuality. Since they were human beings they would inevitably demand recognition as individuals, as persons.

Stone's account of the subordination of the wife from the sixteenth right through to the nineteenth century accords with the legal position we have described. How then can he argue that women gained greater freedom and that the family came to be based on affect in this period? This he can only do within a notion of the nuclear family which 'as a social system . . . has two castes – the male and female – and two classes – adult and child. The male caste always dominates over the female, and the adult class the child, but the latter, if he lives, is guaranteed upward social mobility since in time he becomes an adult' (1977 : 22).

Within the strict limits of such an arrangement perhaps women gained some freedom. Choice of marriage partners came to be allowed, but this was the only increase in woman's freedom. Marriage was the only career open to her. Stone does accept that the shift of motives for marriage from power, status, and money to affection probably worked more to the benefit of men than of women. A successful marriage still depended on the docility of the woman.

Children were also property. (Indeed they still are, although latterly the state has circumscribed parental power.) Children were the property of the husband-father. He was the sole possessor of any children of the marriage and he could remove them from their mother at any time. He could deny her access to them and refuse her knowledge even of their whereabouts. Some changes did take place in the nineteenth century. The Custody of Infants Acts, 1839, allowed that fathers were not owners of children in certain cases. Mothers against whom adultery had not been proved were allowed to keep children under seven years old and to have access to older children. This was further extended in 1873, but equal guardianship was not accorded to both parents until 1925. While these Acts did not remove the status of children as the property of their parents, they did increase the rights of women as mothers.

Practical problems women encountered

The typical bourgeois families of the eighteenth and nineteenth centuries did not constantly quote the law in their day-to-day lives, nor did husbands resort to the wide range of draconian measures to which they were legally entitled. Nevertheless this was the legal framework and in some families it was applied. The story of Elizabeth Barrett Browning is well known. It was cases in which the full rigour of the law was applied that raised the consciousness of some women to their lack of freedom and led

55

them to individual, independent action. This was so in the case of Caroline Norton, who experienced over her life most of the disabilities of a woman's position. Although her consciousness was raised and she took such political and legal action as was available to a nineteenth-century married woman, she did not claim to be a feminist.

Caroline Norton's troubles began when her husband, amid much scandal, sued Lord Melbourne for 'criminal conversation' with his wife. Norton lost the case and Melbourne was acquitted. After the trial Caroline was separated from her husband, who prevented her from seeing her children, even going so far as to refuse her access to one who was dying. In all of this Caroline Norton could take no legal action on her own behalf, for as a married woman she could neither sue nor be sued. Legally she was not a person.

Caroline Norton therefore used other methods to influence the situation, and indeed it was largely as the result of her campaigning that the 1839 Custody of Infants Act was passed. Being utterly without rights she had to use what Strachey has described as the 'weapons of the weak' (Strachey 1978 : 34) namely her beauty, her social position, and her charm. She used the influence that she had through her many aristocratic connections, her literary talents, and the connections she had developed when she had been one of the most successful hostesses of fashionable London, a hostess with whom all the great men of the day loudly professed themselves to be in love.

As we have said, Caroline Norton was a declared anti-feminist. She did not rest her case on any ideological grounds of the 'rights of women'. She found herself driven by the contradictory demands placed upon women. Taught to believe in her duty to love and care for her children, she had found herself without rights to fulfil these duties. These contradictions led her later to agitate for amendments in the law relating to married women's property. She did this because after her separation from her husband, when she was living in her natal home, she had found that her money and property, including her earnings from her writings, continued to be the property of her husband. Despite her great efforts to alleviate the situation of 'wronged women', of separated women, and of women who had been ill-used by their husbands, she repudiated ' "the ill-advised public attempts on the part of a few women to assert 'equality' with 'men' " ', and made fun of ' "strange and laughable political meetings (sanctioned by a chairwoman) which had taken place in one or two instances" ' (Strachey 1978 : 75), for she believed in the natural superiority of men. Thus can her material base drive a woman to a practical position in which she demands revolutionary change without a comparable change in her ideological view.

Changes in the family law

Yet perhaps the changes in family law with which Caroline Norton was involved were not so revolutionary after all. Looking back it seems most likely that these changes were made less in the interests and at the behest of the women than because they were in the interest of capital accumulation as the nature of capitalism changed. Women had been the property of men, and were kept confined in the interests of property and inheritance. As the Lord Chancellor pointed out in a parliamentary debate on the Divorce and Matrimonial Causes Bill, 3 July 1856, on a proposal to set up a divorce court, whereas a wife was not damaged by her husband's adultery and could forgive him 'without any loss of caste' *her* adultery 'might be the means of palming spurious offspring upon the husband' (McGregor 1957 : 10). This would undermine the family through fraud in the succession to its property: these are precisely the same arguments as those that, as we saw in Chapter 3, seem to have been the explanation for the restrictions imposed by the Prophet on women in Islam to ensure that paternity could be known.

But in mid-nineteenth-century England reform was in the air. It began slowly, first recognizing the problems of separated women. Claims made by married women to control their property were thought to be incompatible with marriage. They had, as the *Saturday Review* pointed out ' "a smack of selfish independence about' (them) which rather jars with poetical notions of wedlock" ' (quoted in Strachey 1978 : 75).

In the event, the 1857 Married Women's Property Bill was rejected in favour of the Marriage and Divorce Bill, which became law in 1857 and which made special provision for separated women. This Act allowed for the establishment of a new Court able to direct the payment of maintenance to a wife or her trustee. It also gave a deserted wife protection from claims on her earnings, allowed a wife to inherit and bequeath wealth in the same way as a single woman, and gave a separated wife the power of contract and the power to sue and be sued. Married women still were not persons at law in this regard.

When in 1870 the question of married women's property was again discussed, the resulting Act only allowed women to keep possession of their earnings. This went through because when a woman supported herself from her own earnings it was said to be an 'obvious' injustice if her money was taken from her by a man who had deserted or ill-treated her. This partial success, removing the more blatant excesses of an unjust system, left the reformers to argue the case for married women's property rights from theory and principles of justice.

> 'The "organs" of the (feminist) movement, which had called attention to individual injustices for many years, were thrown back upon theoretical argument, and it soon grew clear that it was not going to be easy, or even possible, to get enthusiastic popular support among men for the remains of the claim.' (Strachey 1978 : 274)

Lord Fraser argued in 1881: 'The protection which has been thrown around a married woman already is sufficient, and why she should be allowed to have money in her pocket to deal with as she thinks fit I cannot understand' (quoted in Strachey 1978 : 275).

But there was some support forthcoming from men. The traders found the existing laws confusing and wished to reduce the possibility of fraud. The propertied classes, also, in the new economic situation, were not happy about their daughters' property being put under the absolute control of their husbands. Money and leaseholds were more significant than land by this time. Sachs and Wilson argue that it was the growth of limited liability companies, creating new forms of economic power divorced from the ownership of the land, that made these reforms possible. They relegated everything to do with the home to the private domestic sphere. Since wealth was no longer land-based it need no longer be family-based, and the merging of a wife's legal being with that of her husband was no longer necessary for capital accumulation (see McGregor, in Sachs and Wilson 1978 : 137).

1882: a triumph for women?

The 1882 Married Women's Property Act is generally regarded as a major development in legal rights for women, because it introduced the concept of separate property rights for husband and wife into English family law. Was it perhaps not such a triumph, yet another step in the privatization of women? Was Caroline Norton correct to say she was not a feminist? The Act implied that women were no longer to be considered as physically or otherwise the property of men. This certainly seems a triumph for feminism. In the opinion of Sachs and Wilson, however, the 1882 Act

> 'did little more than save wealthy women from the irksome restraints of holding property through trustees. In fact, men continued to control the property of women, even if only in the capacity of advisers rather than husbands or trustees, since women were precluded from acquiring the skills thought to be needed for the proper administration of their property, such skills being locked within the male professions.' (Sachs and Wilson 1978 : 137)

The Act, therefore, did not enhance women's power; power remained in the public domain from which they were excluded. Sachs and Wilson go on to argue that, although the Act may have protected women from some abuse in the home, it did not create opportunities for them to be useful outside the home. In their view, indeed, 'the destiny of woman as wife rather than as independent person was enhanced rather than reduced by the Act' since a 'curb on spending by husbands was not the same as a licence to earn independently by wives' (1978 : 137).

The institution of separate property for wives was certainly not seen by contemporaries as destroying complementarity in marriage or replacing it with equality, as the reply of James Fitzjames Stephen to John Stuart Mill in 1873 made plain. It was not until the late 1960s that legislation moving towards a partnership in marriage began to be passed. The responsibility of a husband for his wife's torts and civil wrongs continued for fifty years after the 1882 Act, although during that period cases were brought forward in the Courts which successfully challenged the associated rights of men as to chastisment and custody of a wife's person.

The right to education

While women like Caroline Norton were driven to direct legislative action by the contradictions inherent in the status of women as wives and mothers in nineteenth-century England, others took a broader view. The right of access to education was a subject tackled by the early feminists. They saw the right to education as part of their right to individual personalities, to become more fully 'human beings'. Astell, before 1700, had argued in this way in *A Serious Proposal to the Ladies for the Advancement of their True and Greatest Interest*. Calling herself simply a 'Lover of her Sex', she entreated women to transcend their preoccupation with trivial matters and not to be content to live like tulips in a garden, 'to make a fine show and be good for nothing'. Her serious proposal called for an all-female educational retreat for the pursuit of truth. This was a radical proposal at that time. She tempered it by assuring her readers that she wanted only to improve women's minds. 'We pretend not that women should teach in the Church, or usurp Authority where it is not allowed them' (quoted in Storr 1932 : 25, 26).

In 1739, 'Sophia, a Person of Quality', put her demands for education into a tract, *Woman not Inferior to Man: or a short and modest Vindication of the natural Rights of the Fair Sex to a perfect Equality of Power, Dignity, and Esteem with the Men*. Complaining that men were 'unanimous in thinking, that we are made only for their use, that we are fit only to breed and nurse children in their tender years, to mind household affairs, and to obey, serve, and please our masters . . . themselves' (Sophia 1975 : 11). She went on to say that she thought it was absurd 'to argue that learning is useless to Women, because forsooth they have not a share in public offices, which is the end for which men apply themselves to it.' She saw that the men were having it both ways: 'Why is learning useless to us? Because we have no share in public offices. And why have we no share in public offices? Because we have no learning.' (1975 : 27). All the same Sophia, like Astell, was careful also to say that she had no wish 'to invert the present order of things with regard to government and Authority' (1975 : 56).

Part of Mary Wollstonecraft's quarrel with Rousseau was with his conservative views about women's education. She quotes Rousseau's argument that

> 'the education of women should always be relative to the men. To please, to be useful to us, to make us love and esteem them, to educate us when young, . . . to console us, to render our lives easy and agreeable – these are the duties of women at all times, and what they should be taught in their infancy.' (Wollstonecraft 1975 : 175)

Rousseau thought that women were being taught no more than was consistent with their natural capacities and destiny. It was this belief that Wollstonecraft challenged. A consistent advocate of education, she often justified her appeals for more educational opportunities for women by arguing that a woman, by exercising her mind could become the friend, rather than the humble dependent of her husband. Here is a clear plea to be treated as a person in her own right on an equal basis with a man. A plea which in Stone's view was foolish because it linked educational opportunity with equality of power within the family 'and by so doing destroyed any hope of achieving concrete change' (Stone 1977 : 358).

Education for entry to the public domain: the male opposition

Astell, Sophia, and Wollstonecraft had emphasized the opportunities education would offer women to develop their personalities and to improve their relations with their husbands, that is, their performance in the private, domestic domain. But others were more directly concerned with the public world. As early as 1804 the Ladies' Committee for Providing the Education and Employment of the Female Poor had referred to the lack of education and employment for women. They claimed this state of affairs had been brought about by men's restrictions and

61

argued that justice demanded that women should be restored to occupations for which they were fitted and which had been 'grievously and unjustly intruded upon by the other sex' (quoted in Pinchbeck 1977 : 304–05). Increasingly, the importance of education for women came to be associated with diversification of work for women. By the mid-nineteenth century some bourgeois women were beginning to sense the inherent contra-dictions in the twin ideologies of individualism and familism. The unease and discontent occasioned by this dawning awareness may have been exacerbated by the cheapness and consequent proliferation of domestic servants whom they no longer even had to supervise. Often engaged in respectable philanthropic work, some bourgeois women felt their idleness and redundancy keenly and resentment against useless gentility and futile circumspec-tion grew. Now attention really began to be paid to the men's world and demands for admission to it grew among middle-class women. Thus it was that although in the middle years of the nineteenth century the restriction of women to the home became most marked, it was also at this time that concerted efforts began to be made by women to move out of the home, to share in the education and occupation of the public domain for men. These demands met with some limited success.

Girls were admitted to the Cambridge local examination in 1865 and to Oxford in 1870, but unlike boys they were not placed in order of merit, but simply given a pass or fail. London Univer-sity examinations were opened to women in 1878 but they con-tinued to be barred from the medical school. Women's colleges started about the same time: Girton in 1870 and Newnham in 1871. Even in these establishments the debate continued as to whether women should have the same education as men or whether it should be less openly competitive.

It was when a demand for education was associated with entry to an occupation hitherto the exclusive domain of men that the opposition was strongest. Such was the case with the medical schools. The struggles of Elizabeth Garrett Anderson and Sophia Blake for medical education and for registration encountered the most astonishingly implacable male opposition. When the women tried to assert their rights at law the judge painted a picture of women as being too delicate and refined to undertake

62

public functions. Sachs and Wilson, who have carefully documented the consistent resistance of men to women's emancipation, quote Lord Neaves who argued in 1873 that

> ' "there is a great difference in the mental constitution of the two sexes, just as there is in their physical conformation. The powers and susceptibilities of women are as noble as those of men; but they are thought to be different, and, in particular, it is considered that they have not the same power of intense labour as men are endowed with." ' (quoted in Sachs and Wilson 1978 : 18)

For these reasons they should not study medicine and if they did they would pull down average standards. ' "Add to this" ', his Lordship continued,

> ' "the special acquirements and accomplishments at which women must aim, but from which men may easily remain exempt (sic). Much time must, or ought to be, given by women to the acquisition of a knowledge of household affairs and family duties, as well as those ornamental parts of education which tends so much to social refinement and domestic happiness, and the study necessary for mastering these must always form a serious distraction from severer pursuits . . ." ' (quoted in Sachs and Wilson 1978 : 18)

It was the argument that women were too delicate and refined to undertake public functions, rather than an argument that women were too busy nursing, that was used to support the view that women should be excluded from the public world. The consequence of this protective attitude was to classify women legally alongside the insane, the insolvent, and the inanimate (Sachs and Wilson 1978 : 6). The male monopoly cases demonstrate in the view of Sachs and Wilson 'a gender bias so striking and so explicit as to contradict totally the idea of judicial impartiality' (1978 : 7). This idea therefore seems to be yet another myth. The male-dominated judiciary was sustaining the gender order, the judiciary was by no means neutral. Indeed, the long history of legal opposition to women's emancipation can only be explained by the idea that men were acting as a group (cf. Davidoff 1977). The men in the legal profession acted to support the men in the medical profession, although to this day the legal profession remains more intransigent towards women than even the medical profession.

Despite their proclamation of the equality of men, based on common humanity, it was in the interests of men, who had sole occupancy of the prestigious and powerful positions that 'man' should be interpreted as 'male'. Part of the battle that women had to fight in their attempt to enter the public domain was simply that they should be recognized as persons, as human beings, and as individuals who had equal rights with men before the law. It was not until 1929 that women were finally accepted as 'persons' at law, when the British Privy Council ruled that they were eligible to stand for the Canadian Senate. While that ruling was not binding in Britain, a great deal of attention would have been paid to it in a British court. Never since has a woman been denied access to any position on the sole ground that she was not a 'person'.

While men denied the personhood, the individuality of women, on the grounds of their domestic tasks and their associated female nature, women were much slower to see their familial roles as a source of their own oppression. The dominant ideology of the nineteenth century connected women's place as wife and mother, their natural capacities, and the stability and morality of society. Many women as well as men shared the views expressed by Lord Neaves that women were too delicate for the rigours of academic life, that education would put an unbearable strain on them, causing nervous troubles and endangering their productive ability. Spencer suggested that flat-chested girls, after a period of higher education, would be unable to suckle infants (Marks 1976 : 189).

These same spokesmen overlooked the realities of life for working-class women where long hours of heavy work were the rule: heavy work in the home for all, and for many, heavy work in waged labour as well. When the 1870 Education Act made schooling available for all children up to the age of ten, in so far as the education of working-class girls was thought about at all, it was to be no more than a rudimentary education. Even so, girls and boys were educated differently at this level. The idea of a 'vocational' education for working-class children, to prepare them for their place in life, led to a curriculum for girls that included housecrafts – both to ensure the future exercise of thrift with their own families and to prepare them for entry into domestic service.

Education only one step

Wollstonecraft, at the end of the eighteenth century, had been a consistent advocate of education for women, but she saw that more than education and the incorporation of women into existing society was going to be needed for the full emancipation of women: 'till society be differently constituted, much cannot be expected from education' (Wollstonecraft 1975 : 67). And again, 'I do not believe that a private education can work the wonders which some sanguine writers have attributed to it. Men and women must be educated, in a great degree, by the opinions and manners of the society they live in' (Wollstonecraft 1975 : 102).

With hindsight we can see that Wollstonecraft was quite right: a good deal more than education is necessary to liberate women. At the same time these early feminists were correct to point to the importance of education. The lack of education for women was one way in which women were oppressed. Furthermore, as we shall see later, in a greatly disadvantaged position compared with men, it has been educated women who have been among those who have made the most use of the vote. Education proved to be one of the few resources that twentieth-century women had in their own right. At the same time it has been educated women in the second half of the twentieth century who have felt their continued oppression most keenly and most articulately. In the eighteenth and nineteenth centuries the notion that they were persons who should have civil and political rights was gradually dawning on women, and was bitterly opposed by most, but not all, men.

The problem of the spinsters

Oppression by a husband, whose justification was found in the familial system and in male domination, was what motivated such different women as Wollstonecraft and Norton. The failure of the Victorian nuclear family to find a satisfactory place for them was what led other women to action and men to reforms on their behalf. A surplus of women developed in mid-century. Emigration, wars, a tendency for girl babies to survive better than boys, all combined to produce a surplus of women over men. Aggravated by the tendency of men to delay marriage in the new economic situation, with the expenses involved in maintaining a wife and family in the new bourgeois pattern, the problem of the spinsters arose. The problems presented by these unsupported women increased the demands for education and occupation for women.

It was estimated by mid-century that one woman out of three was engaged in separate industry (Stone quotes a figure of 25 per cent (1977 : 7)):

> 'There are hundreds and thousands of women . . . scattered through all ranks, but proportionately most numerous in the middle and upper classes – who have to earn their own living, instead of spending and husbanding the earnings of men; who, not having the natural (sic) duties and labours of wives and mothers, have to carve out artificial and painfully-sought occupations for themselves; who, in place of completing, sweetening and embellishing the existence of others, are compelled to lead an independent and incomplete existence of their own.' (Greg 1877)

It was quite clear that such women were failures and often dealt with unsympathetically. Thus the *Saturday Review* commented:

> 'Married life is a woman's profession; and to this life her training – that of dependence – is modelled. Of course, by not getting a husband, or losing him, she may find she is without resources. All that can be said of her is, she has failed in business and no social reform can prevent such failures.' (quoted in Strachey 1978 : 92)

It was in this environment that Florence Nightingale reformed nursing and established nurse training for women. She founded the new nursing strictly within the gender order of her society, establishing matrons in charge of hospitals in the same way as aristocratic and bourgeois wives were in charge of Victorian households: in command of the servants (thus oppressing other women) but subservient to the men, male doctors replacing the patriarchal head of the Victorian family. In calling women out of the home she may have deplored the 'petty grinding tyranny of a good English family' (Woodham-Smith 1950 : 93), but she established something remarkably like it in her hospitals (Austin 1976; Carpenter 1977 : 167–68).

Women reinforcing the class structure

At this time too the new Ladies Bountiful emerged, those upper- and middle-class women who found outlets for their energies, which were not needed in the household, in social and charitable work. Louisa Twining became involved with workhouse conditions, Baroness Burdett Coutts used her own fortune in support of many charitable causes; Mary Carpenter founded Reformatory Schools and worked for governmental action in regard to juvenile delinquency; Octavia Hill worked for the improvement of housing conditions for the poor and initiated a system of housing management by trained women. In Disraeli's 'two nations' philanthropic work was established as a suitable occupation for ladies. Many of the recipients were also women. While no doubt the concern of many was to do good, nevertheless this development has to be seen as one in which women were supporting their husbands in the maintenance of the class system and extending the notions of the bourgeois family to the working class (cf. bourgeois women in India today (Caplan 1978)).

Such values informed the work of many who became interested in 'rescue work', in the plight of unsupported women who had failed in the marriage market, and in 'fallen women', many being especially concerned with prostitution. Josephine Butler was unusual among these good ladies for her recognition of the sex and class power of middle- and upper-class men and their responsibility for the problems which beset women. She campaigned against the Contagious Diseases Act which was designed to prevent venereal diseases in the armed forces. It provided for the summary medical inspection of suspected prostitutes in garrison towns. She recognized the implied slur on all working-class women and condemned the hypocrisy of middle- and upper-class men without whose custom the prostitute could not operate. Her campaign for the repeal of the Act went beyond the boundaries of more conventional rescue and challenged the established power and authority of the men. Consequently, the campaign was greeted with distaste and outrage in respectable circles.

Apart from the few like Josephine Butler, the philanthropic campaigns epitomized respectability and were charitable rather than emancipated. The reformers did not make radical criticisms of existing institutions. They called instead on men to behave in ways consistent with their duties towards the 'weaker sex', and upon men in the legislature to make new laws consistent with these duties. The weaker sex themselves, who were rather contradictorally constituted by the same social order as the guardians of morality, had to justify their excursions into certain public spheres, their departures from 'woman's place'. Women made these excursions particularly around issues like temperance, child prostitution, and slavery. Their justification was the manifest need to bring women's civilizing influence to bear on a harsh world and to 'humanize' society. While the charitable movement brought some women out of the home, it did not for the most part lead them to challenge the male hegemony. Indeed, like the Married Women's Property Act, it could be said to have reinforced a new form of the male hegemony. Release from one set of irksome constraints in the longer run revealed the more underlying constraints.

The demand for the vote

It is not surprising that, faced with continual opposition to their claims, women in the second half of the nineteenth century should have demanded the vote. This was the individualistic right that had been accorded to bourgeois men and had liberated them to some extent at least from the domination of the aristocracy. The women saw in the denial of the vote the withholding of the key which would release them from enforced domesticity, inferior education, and lack of professional opportunities. In Rowbotham's words: 'If women could vote they could change man-made laws' (Rowbotham 1974b : 50).

For many centuries previously the question of whether women should have the vote had not arisen. In the feudal period when persons were merged into their families and kin groups the question of individual votes was not imaginable. Government, like property owning, was on a family, that is to say a kin, basis. Generally speaking the male head of the group represented all its members and was responsible for them. Occasionally women stood in for their husbands in governmental as in other matters. Millicent Fawcett believed that in feudal times 'women exercised electoral rights in those cases where they were entitled as landowners or freewomen of certain towns to do so' (Fawcett 1912 : 8). In any case, as we have seen, it was only a tiny minority of the population who were involved in substantial property rights or in government. It is doubtless this occasional exercise on behalf of a family or kin group by women, in the manner in which Elizabeth had ascended the throne in 1533, that led later campaigners to believe that there had been a golden age when women shared in the responsibilities of government. Roger Fulford records that in the view of the nineteenth-century campaigners for the franchise, 'Votes for women was a Paradise which women had once possessed, had now lost and must regain' (Fulford 1976 : 20). As hard evidence Mrs Fawcett quotes the *Annals of a Yorkshire House* which records that the 'womenfolk need not vote' because the candidate was certain of success (Fawcett 1912 : 8–9). Abbesses had received summonses to attend the earliest Parliaments and some women who were large landowners had been able to control local elections, Anne, Countess of Dorset in the seventeenth century, perhaps being the most effective. In the reign of James I it was ruled that a spinster who was a freeholder could 'vote for a Parliament man'. In the eighteenth century in a case following the contested election of Sarah Bly as sexton to a City church, a judge reiterated that there was 'no disability in a woman from voting for a Parliament man'. Final judgment accepted Sarah Bly's election to the parochial position on the grounds that 'it does not seem a thing of public consideration in which I incline to think that women have not a right of voting, though they are not positively excluded' (quoted in Fulford 1976 : 22). These examples hardly constituted evidence for a past golden age of women's political powers.

As notions of individualism and of independent personhood were gaining ground, the question of women voting became a serious issue. And it was then that they were specifically excluded. It was in the Reform Act of 1832 that the prefix 'male' was included when enumerating persons entitled to vote. In 1797 Fox asked why it had never been imagined that women should have the vote and concluded that nature and convention had made ' "that sex dependent on ours" and that therefore "their voices would be governed by the relations in which they stand to society" ' (Fulford 1976 : 23). The threat to those relations which were implied by the rising individualism led to the reinforcement of the patriarchal relations. It became necessary to state women's disqualifications for government. As James Mill wrote in his celebrated 1824 *Essay on Government*:

> 'one thing is pretty clear, that all those individuals whose interests are indisputably included in those of other individuals may be struck off from political rights without inconvenience. . . . In this light . . . women may be regarded, the interest of almost all of whom is involved in that of their fathers or in that of their husbands.' (Mill 1937 : 45, quoted in Fulford 1976 : 26–7)

Property more important than sex

Mill's article provoked a response from William Thompson: *An Appeal of One Half of the Human Race, Women, against the Pretension of the other Half, Men, to retain them in Political, and thence in Civil and Domestic Slavery* (1825). Thompson's work was largely ignored until restated in part years later by John Stuart Mill (see Pankhurst 1954). In 1832 Mr Hunt presented a petition to the reformed Parliament on behalf of Mary Smith, a wealthy property owner, requesting that 'every unmarried female possessing the necessary pecuniary qualification should be entitled to vote for Members of Parliament'. In making the presentation, Hunt commented that it 'might be a subject of mirth to some hon. gentlemen, but (it) was one deserving consideration' (quoted in Strachey 1978 : 32).

The arguments that were emerging were that property was the qualification for being involved in government, and it was incorrect that property owners should be disenfranchised in consequence of their sex. These arguments continued to be a persistent theme throughout the nineteenth century and were continually made in campaigns over the extension of the municipal franchise to women householders which was finally granted in 1870. The *feme sole* had, after all, always had rather different rights in England from her married sister.

As we saw in the last chapter the demand for universal adult suffrage was one of the foundations of the Chartist movement which at the outset specifically included the franchise for women. We saw how ambiguous the Chartists were about women, later shelving the demand for women's franchise for fear it might prejudice the movement's principal aim: to gain the vote for the workers (male).

The celebrated Black Book, which included all the radical and some revolutionary ideals of the 1830s, argued that an unlimited scheme of universal suffrage could not be seriously entertained since it would include women as well as men. 'If asked why disenfranchise women in preference to men we confess, in answer, to these enquiries we can only give one reply, namely, that expediency, not strict justice, dictates their exclusion' (Wade 1835 : 602, quoted in Fulford 1976 : 33).

The suffrage movement develops

By mid-century, John Stuart Mill was asking for political power for *a woman in her own right*. In the sixties the frustrations experienced by women attempting to enter the professions, the growing awareness of the absurd position of many middle- and upper-class women and of single women, and the recognition of the limits that propriety placed on women's contribution to philanthropic causes mingled with the growing clamour for Parliamentary reform. The first woman's suffrage committee met to support John Stuart Mill's election as member of Parliament for Westminster. In response, suffrage societies sprang up in Manchester, Edinburgh, Bristol, and Birmingham. A recognizable movement was developing. The extent to which this movement was drawing together women who were working in various ways for the entry of women into the public domain is illustrated by the people who attended a meeting held by the Kensington Society, later reconstituted as the London National Society for Women's Suffrage. The society held a meeting in 1865 to discuss women's right to participate in public affairs, a paper being presented on the suffrage. Among those present were Emily Davies, a pioneer of education for women, Dorothea Beale, later principal of Cheltenham Ladies College, Frances Mary Buss, founder of the North London Collegiate School for Girls and co-founder of the Headmistresses Association, Elizabeth Garrett Anderson, fighting to open the medical profession to women, Jessie Boucherett, founder of the Society for Promoting the Employment of Women, Barbara Bodichon, daughter of a radical MP cousin of Florence Nightingale and agitator for the Married Women's Property Acts (Strachey 1978 : 103).

In the context in which the 1867 Conservative government were forced to put through the Liberal claims for the enfranchisement of some working men, Mill put forward his now famous amendment for the enfranchisement of certain qualified women based entirely on liberal principles of individualism:

> 'It is said that women do not need direct power, having so much indirect, through their influence over their male relatives and connections. I should like to carry this argument a little further. Rich people have a great deal of indirect influence. Is this a reason for refusing them votes?. . . Sir, it is true that women . . . have great power; but they have it under the worst possible conditions, because it is indirect, and therefore irresponsible power. . . . But at least, it will be said, women do not suffer any practical inconvenience, as women, by not having a vote. The interests of all women are safe in the hands of their husbands and brothers, who have the same interest with them. . . . Sir, this is exactly what is said of all unrepresented classes. The operatives, for instance: are they not virtually represented by the representation of their employers?. . . and generally, have not employers and employed a common interest against all outsiders, just as husband and wife have against all outside the family? And what is more, are not all employers good, kind, benevolent men, who love their work people, and always desire to do what is most for their

72

good? All these assertions are as true, and as much to the purpose, as the corresponding assertions respecting men and women. Sir, we do not live in Arcadia . . . and workmen need other protection than that of their employers, and women other protection than that of their men.' (*Hansard* 1867, quoted in Strachey 1978 : 108)

In practice, had the amendment been passed the female franchise would have been limited largely to widows and affluent spinsters. In the eyes of *The Times* this would mean

'perpetuating the disenfranchisement of married ladies who are not separated from their husbands, and of young ladies who are not orphans, admits to the polling booth a mixed multitude of widows and those whom, for want of a more respectful term, we must needs call old maids.' (*The Times* 21 May 1867, quoted in Fulford 1976 : 70)

Mill's amendment was not passed. But the suffrage movement was now well under way. Almost immediately the organizers capitalized on a chance occurrence when the name of a Mrs Maxwell slipped on to the register of Parliamentary voters. In a by-election in 1867 she went amid much support to the poll and recorded her vote. In the following year over five thousand women householders of Manchester took their case for enfranchisement before the Court of Common Pleas. This was followed by a nationwide campaign to enlist the support of new Members of Parliament to redress the Court's adverse verdict. Women, rewarded by ridicule and charges of unfemininity, learned the arts of organizing and addressing public meetings. But the 1870 Suffrage Bill met with determined and unexplained opposition from Gladstone at the committee stage. Almost half a century was to pass before any women were able to vote in Parliamentary elections.

During this time the movement continued, but not surprisingly it was not united. The reasons which had led women into the movement were various as we have seen, their priorities and their dominant goals differed. Some felt that Josephine Butler's crusade against the Contagious Diseases Act brought unpleasant notoriety to the cause. Later a group of women broke away from the main movement in exasperation with the bad faith and broken promises of one government after another. Under the leadership of Emmeline and Christabel Pankhurst they formed the militant suffrage movement, existing in an uneasy alliance with the Independent Labour Party. Members took direct action and were prepared to be martyred for the cause. They endured imprisonment, hunger strikes, and force feeding. In the meantime Mrs Fawcett led the remains of the main movement denouncing the unconstitutional methods of the militants and continuing their unremitting, constitutional campaign to educate public opinion (cf. Kamm 1966; Pankhurst 1977).

Party leaders were afraid to accede to the women's claims, although in some Parliaments there were majorities in favour of female suffrage. They were afraid of the political consequences of votes for women. 'The Liberals were convinced that women would vote Conservative, and the Conservatives felt sure that they would vote Liberal; and neither side cared enough about the matter to take this appalling risk' (Strachey 1978 : 266). In 1911, Asquith remained as unyielding as had Gladstone, believing that the inclusion of women in the franchise would be a 'political mistake of a very disastrous kind'. Thus it was not until 1918 and after a major contribution to the effort of the 1914–18 War that women over thirty were granted the vote, almost ninety years after they had been formally disenfranchised. And another decade passed before a full franchise was accorded to all women.

In all this long struggle women had been concerned with their rights as individuals. They had not paid attention to the institution of the family other than to support it, except in so far as family law had limited their freedom. They had not been concerned with the restrictions on their lives occasioned by their role as child-rearers and housewives. Indeed, all the feminist utterances were in support of the family and the virtues of motherhood. In this they followed the tradition set by Wollstonecraft, of whom as Jo and Olive Banks point out, 'Nowhere in [her] book does Wollstonecraft complain of the burdens the wife and mother has to carry in the fulfilment of her maternal duties' (1964 : 16). These of course had not borne so heavily on the middle-class leaders of the movement, one of whose problems was their lack of work; servants did their housework. The problem was not to come home to the middle class until servants became increasingly difficult to find after the First World War and almost completely disappeared after the Second.

FIVE

Suffrage without emancipation

'Sixty years ago . . . the male monopoly of Parliament was broken when the first woman MP took her seat in the House of Commons. Ten years later there was a woman Cabinet Minister, and now we have a woman Prime Minister. All things considered, women have advanced very rapidly in British politics since 1 December 1919, and all who believe in sexual equality should be grateful to the woman who achieved the historic breakthrough – Nancy Astor . . . [In 1946 her husband] decided it was essential for her to withdraw. His health had collapsed and he knew that he would not be able to help her, as in the past. So just before the twenty-fifth anniversary of her entry into Parliament he wrote to the Divisional Tories to say that she would not be standing again.' (John Grigg, *The Observer*, 25 November 1979)

Suffrage as a recognition of the individuality of women

What the nineteenth and early twentieth-century feminists had been arguing for was acceptance as individuals who should have the power to act in their own right, not just as mothers, daughters, or wives. They were arguing for entry to the public domain, yet they did not wish to cease to be mothers, daughters, or wives, although increasingly they sought to control their own fertility, feeling as Queen Victoria had written to her uncle, that they did not want to be 'mamam d'une grande famille'. Thus the basis of feminism was individualism and self-determination, and a wish therefore to be involved in those public power structures that determined so much about the status of women and the life of the family. In the feminist movement of the eighteenth and nineteenth centuries elements of rationalism, liberal individualism, and historical materialism mingled. The notion of the inalienable rights of the individual with which the principle of equality was associated derived from the eighteenth-century rationalists. This notion had first been brought to bear on women's problems by Mary Wollstonecraft and remained closely associated with the suffrage demands.

The demand for adult female suffrage was a demand for political recognition of this utterly new status for women as individuals who could act in their own right, and who could enter the public world as individuals rather than as members of families. This was indeed a radical demand. The extent of its radicalism and the nature of other changes that would be needed to achieve equal individual status with men were not recognized by the early feminists.

Acceptance of the family

Despite their individualistic radicalism, women in the suffrage movement were conservative about the family. Perhaps they could not have been otherwise given the economic and social mores of their day. Hindsight makes criticism easy. Early suffragists accepted the place of women in the family and the gender roles and the division of labour that went with it. It is only latterly that feminists have come to recognize how many other changes

77

are needed if women are to share power with men. In the late twentieth century they have recognized that the gender order must alter in the private as well as the public domain if women are to be fully emancipated, with men undertaking 'women's work' as much as women doing 'men's'.

Political equality without civil equality

Not only was the feminist demand radical, but the process of emancipation for women was different from that for men, as we saw in the last chapter. One might say that women reversed the path to citizenship already taken by men. Men had fought for civil and political rights from positions in the public world and from their individual statuses there. They had eventually gained political rights in order to consolidate and safeguard those public interests. The growth of civil rights had been, as we saw, indispensable to the development of a competitive market economy. While there were great inequalities in the bargaining power of capital and labour, their relationship had a rational-legal basis, being based on contracts which could be made or broken. This was not so in the case of the relationships between men and women based on marriage. In previous history whenever women had exercised power or influence they had done so as members of families. They had had to fight for political rights and legal reforms through men, for they had no public positions of their own. Apart from the family, they had no power bases from which to proceed in their attempt to enter the public domain.

Although there were always differences between single and widowed women and their married sisters, we have argued that women gained elements of political citizenship before they were finally accepted as persons at law. And even when they were finally accepted as persons at law, men continued to exclude them from many places in the public domain until well into the second half of the twentieth century.

The continued importance of the family

Thus it was from their family membership, or despite their family membership as the case might be, that women had to try to

78

translate their newly found political citizenship into political action. Any resources that women were able to command derived principally from their family membership. Some, it is true, had education in their own right, which proved to be a valuable resource, but those who could achieve a good education, especially at the start of the century, came from the more privileged families. Family membership, or inheritance therefrom, was important for the *feme sole* as it was for the married woman, although the *feme sole* had more freedom than her married sister to use any wealth she had inherited as she wished. It was the married state, as we saw in the last chapter, that was so constraining, and so it continued to be. Initially the constraints were legal, but custom continued to bind women even when the legal restraints were reduced. Women were not only the child-bearers but also the child-rearers, so that even when they had political equality they did not have social equality. Women continued to think of themselves primarily as wives and mothers, and the men encouraged them in this. It was not in the interests of men as a group to support women in their bid for power and position outside the family, although individual liberally-minded men did so. Men as a social group stood to lose both from the increased competition of women in the public domain and from the loss of their services in the family should women claim full equality and independence. In the event, men were able to ensure that women only had a secondary role in public affairs for a further half century: this the men could do because only a small minority of women were able to compete *on equal terms* with men in the public world.

It is significant that many of the suffrage movement's most prominent and enthusiastic members were less constrained than most women by their traditional family status. Many of them were single and educated women from middle- and upper-class families.

As Liddington and Norris (1978) point out, most accounts of the suffrage movement have concentrated on the activities of the national leadership, especially on the accounts of the Pankhursts. Undoubtedly the first decade of the twentieth century was dominated by the visibility of the militant suffragettes of the Women's Social and Political Union (WSPU). Their attacks on

79

property, their ability to stage-manage protest and to exploit publicity, the sufferings and courage of their members, their eventual clandestine and authoritarian headquarters in Paris, was good copy for contemporary newspapers and could be retold dramatically to subsequent generations. The less sensational methods of the giant non-militant National Union of Women's Suffrage Societies (NUWSS) led by Mrs Fawcett received less attention, both then and now. Adela Kensington, Barbara Wootton's mother, is one example of a woman 'conservative and conventional' in politics and religion, but who nevertheless held regular suffrage meetings in her house 'but they were always attended only by strict constitutionalists' (Wootton 1967 : 20–1).

Working-class women in politics

The part played by working-class women has also been under-estimated in most accounts of the suffrage movement. Working-class women had been active in political agitation in the early part of the nineteenth century but in mid-century they appeared to have retreated to the private domain. By the end of the century and in the twentieth century they became politically active again. Liddington and Norris report how difficult it is to get information about the struggles of 'the tens of thousands of women in suffrage societies up and down the country who backed the demand for the vote. We know little about the working class women . . . who were active in the campaign; we know even less about their reasons for wanting the vote' (1978 : 13, 14).

The 'radical suffragists' of the North of England, of whom Liddington and Norris write, organized among the textile workers of Lancashire (where for many years women had worked in paid labour). Painstakingly they tried to build a broad, democratic movement among the mass of women. They fought on a wide range of issues, not only for the vote; they called for equal pay, better educational opportunities, birth control, family allowances, and the right to work. Their campaign, rooted in the experiences of working-class women in the family and in the mill, was in marked contrast to that of the militant and bourgeois-dominated WSPU with its single goal of 'Votes for Women'.

80

Working-class women were involved in a double struggle as workers and as workers' wives, not only as women. Lucy Middleton has recorded how, during the opening decade of the twentieth century, there was a growing desire among working-class women for more knowledge about Labour's struggles and for a larger share in the work for Labour emancipation (1977 : 24). Wives and families were affected by the industrial strife and political problems surrounding the rise of the 'new unionism'. 'It is not really surprising', she goes on, 'that the demand for women to have a chance to know more of Labour politics should have come initially from two trade union sources – from the wives of railway workers and from a docker's wife in Hull' (Middleton 1977 : 24). The latter, Mrs Cawthorne, feeling that women 'had a right to know what their men were fighting for' (Middleton 1977 : 25), wrote to Ramsay MacDonald, then the secretary of the National Labour Representation Committee. In their turn he and his assistant consulted their wives.

Acceptance of their role as wives and mothers

From these and similar initiatives the first conference of the Women's Labour League took place in 1906. The early feminists had not challenged the role of women as wives and mothers, indeed they had actively supported it. So did the labour women of the early twentieth century. There was thus this central paradox in the women's campaigns: they wanted freedom as persons and as individuals to enter the public domain and at the same time they wanted the family strengthened. One of the reasons for wanting the vote was to be able to influence those policies which so affected the family. From the outset the paradox between women acting as individual citizens and as wives and mothers emerged centrally in the arguments of the movement, as the following two excerpts from speeches of Margaret MacDonald, which Middleton quotes, make plain. In 1906, outlining the objectives of the new Labour women's organization Margaret MacDonald said:

'We want to show the wives of trade unionists and co-operators, particularly, what they have not yet fully dis-

81

covered, that the best way of looking after their homes is by taking an interest in the life of the community . . . that to improve their conditions it is necessary to take up their cause with earnestness on the same lines as men have done.' (quoted in Middleton 1977 : 25–6)

The following year, MacDonald made the paradox particularly clear when she argued that the movement could not rely for progress solely upon the activities of those women who could more easily take part in public life: 'the great majority of women whose *first duty and responsibility is to their home and children* are learning that they cannot fulfil their charge without taking part in civic life which surrounds and vitally affects their home life' (quoted in Ferguson 1977 : 41, our emphasis). What she and many subsequent Labour women overlooked was that it was precisely their position as wives and mothers which prevented many women from taking up politics on the 'same lines as men have done'.

Probably it was inevitable that arguments should be made in these terms, for this was where the women were: their material base was in the home, the preferred status was that of married women. Probably one should not expect that they could have questioned the division of labour more fundamentally at that time than to suggest that women should take an interest in the affairs of the public world, hitherto, at least since the demise of Chartism, totally dominated by men.

Hannah Mitchell's autobiography (1977) reveals the frustrations of a working-class girl growing up in the 1870s and denied education. The autobiography shows her emergence through the suffragette movement to become ultimately a county councillor. She reveals how irked she is at the domestic dependence of men upon women, but it is interesting to whom she turned to help her become free of the trammels of the family. It was friendly *women* neighbours, many of whom did not believe in the vote, who gave her husband his tea. It was the niece who lived with them later whom she trained to take her place when she was away politicking, not her son. Nor did she leave her husband to fend for himself. He, sympathetic though he was to the Cause, obviously felt he was doing enough just taking his already-prepared tea out of the oven. At one point she records that she realized later she should have insisted more on his sharing the domestic responsibilities (Mitchell 1977 : 100).

The suffragettes were concerned that the family should not be undermined. Hilary Land (1976) has reminded us that Mrs Pankhurst and Millicent Fawcett were against family allowances because they believed they would weaken parental authority. Labour women and suffragettes and suffragists alike thought that women could claim their full citizenship without disrupting the family. The anti-suffragists were not so sure. They sensed and feared the extent of the transformation that any real measure of emancipation for women would require.

Women in the Women's Labour League, the Women's Co-operative Guild, and the trade unions saw everywhere around them simply the need to improve the conditions of family life and of the employment of women. Issues raised included the pay and conditions of women's work, sweated labour, infant medical care, school meals, medical inspection and treatment for school children, and the provision of pithead baths. The radical suffragists who recognized that those of them who were married with children were fighting with 'one hand tied behind them' were most concerned about how to ease the burdens of what later came to be called 'women's two roles', wife-mother and wage-worker. None of them challenged the division of labour in the family. By 1965, although still accepting the family, Ramelson (1967) was proposing changes in the domestic division of labour.

The intrusion of the state into the family

The labour women's movement saw some real achievements resulting from these demands, ranging from the establishment of a model baby clinic in 1911 to the Maternity and Child Welfare Act of 1918. Another interpretation would see these developments as the imposition of middle-class notions upon the working class and as part of the increasing invasion of the private domain by representatives of the public domain. What had begun as a voluntary movement of the Ladies Bountiful to instruct the poor in better ways of child-rearing and home management, i.e. in values and practices acceptable to the middle class, were by the twentieth century becoming official government policy and increasingly being undertaken by persons, such as health visitors, employed by local government. This state interest in the way mothers rear their children did not then, and has not since, increased the importance of family welfare as a topic for debate in the public domain (cf. Wilson 1977; Cockburn 1977 : 58–62). Such topics were and are trivialized as being women's concerns and belonging to the private domain. Nor has state intervention in these areas of women's business led to any marked increase in the number of women in the highest levels of national government where so much is done to determine the conditions of family life.

This increased concern of the state in the welfare of the family by no means derived solely from the social democratic demands of the labour movement: great anxiety had been expressed at the poor state of the nation's health at the time of the Boer War. Government was anxious that the nation's children should grow up fit to fight. The consequent legislation to improve family welfare was predicated upon the central role of women in the family as wife and mother. Neither the feminist nor the socialist movements of the period challenged this. Both accepted the centrality of the family to the society and of women to the family.

The uneasy relationship between socialism and feminism

For Margaret Cole, becoming a socialist in 1911 meant that she 'naturally became at the same time a feminist' (Cole 1949 : 43). But in general, the relationship between socialism and feminism was an uneasy one. Even in that period when feminism was concentrating on votes for women there were mutual suspicions between Labour and the supporters of the suffrage movement. Many middle-class women, including the Pankhursts, had been drawn towards the Labour movement in the 1890s, but there were difficulties. Both the NUWSS and the WSPU advocated votes for women on the same terms as men, which at the beginning of the twentieth century meant votes based on property or occupation. Labour was opposed to any measure that would advantage the middle and upper classes. On the other side, the feminists felt that their interests were constantly in danger of being sold out in favour of the workers' vote. The divisions between the women's suffragists and the adult suffragists dominated the complex and shifting alignments of the 1900s. Liddington and Norris (1978) have documented the agonizing dilemmas of many radical suffragists caught between accusations of 'sex prejudice' and counter-accusations of 'class prejudice' which continued throughout the decade.

The illusory unity of the women's movement

The women's movement had been united around the liberal feminist demand for the vote. This unity, as Sheila Rowbotham points out, was almost illusory. At various times, individuals and groups differed over strategy and tactics, they were divided by political loyalties and the issue of war. Above all, their hopes were divergent:

> 'A suffragette in the Conservative and Unionist Party said it would be a means of ending the White Slave traffic and reducing prostitution. Mrs Pethick Lawrence thought women would be able to reform prisons, improve wardresses' conditions, and transform the economic helplessness of the unsupported mother. Mrs Pankhurst said it would help to end sweated work and improve the training of midwives. Other supporters of women's suffrage . . . (believed) that the vote would see women on the road to equal pay!' (Rowbotham 1974b : 82)

Consequently, when the vote was partially achieved and women over thirty were given the vote in 1918, the movement collapsed. There was no other coherent, organizational basis and no other set of common interests to fall back on. The leadership disbanded. The WSPU closed down and its leaders dispersed to pursue other causes. The constitutional liberal feminists fought on, changing the name of their organization to the National Union of Societies for Equal Citizenship (NUSEC) for 'equality ("real equality of liberties, status and opportunities") and educating women in "the duties of citizenship"' (Gardiner 1976 : 61). Until 1928 they continued to work for the franchise for all adult women and, later, to remove inequalities between the sexes in divorce, inheritance and marriage laws, the guardianship of children, employment opportunities, and rates of pay.

In 1928 the feeling that the main fight was won was strong. Ray Strachey, although she realised that legal reforms were not the whole story, nevertheless wrote 'the main fight is over, and the main victory is won. With education, enfranchisement, and legal equality all conceded, the future of women lies in their own hands' (Strachey 1978 : 385).

Why did the women's movement collapse? Why had there been such a miscellaneous array of goals? Why indeed was there no women's party? Some of the suffragists had hoped for a women's party which would attack the male ways of doing things and upset the (men-only) system of government. A pamphlet of 1918 declared:

' "While the Women's Party is in no way based on sex antagonism it is felt that women can best serve the nation by keeping clear of men's party political machines and traditions, which, by universal consent, leave so much to be desired." ' (quoted in Brookes 1967 : 9)

but Mrs Pankhurst's efforts to found such a party met with very limited and shortlived success.

Women divided by family and by class

There is a sense in which all women had a common material base. There was a communality about housework and family duties which all women shared. But each woman was attached to a family and the material bases of their families in the public world derived from the class position in that world of the husband-father; women were divided by their allegiance to their separate family interests as defined by their husbands. Some working-class women experienced the alienated conditions of wage labour as did their husbands, although often their interests differed from those of the men. But their material differences from their middle-class sisters were even greater. Those women did not directly experience the world of work. Women were not in industrial management at the start of the century, but they shared their husband's class interests; it was by employing other women to work for them in the home that they were able to spend so much time in political activity.

The women in service may have appreciated what was going on, but at least one of them did not find it relevant for her condition. Lucretia Cromwell, a fenwoman, was a widow of seventy-six at the time she recalled:

> 'When they got the vote, the women, they worked hard for it, I suppose. I was in London at the time, in service. They chained themselves to the railings and that. But I wasn't that pleased to get it. Well, it didn't really worry me. I'm not a rebel. It didn't affect country people. It were only in the cities, really. . . . You see, in the country, women didn't bother about the vote, not round here. We liked to know women had got the voting. That women were considered as fine as were the men. They could see more, really, being a woman, couldn't they?' (Chamberlain 1975 : 132)

Yet Mrs Cromwell was undoubtedly politically aware. In her fen village women worked as agricultural labourers and their material dependence on their husbands meant that the politics of class rather than of sex took precedence. Mrs Cromwell described how the working people in her village were Liberal in opposition to the Conservative farmers and the pressure put on them by the farmers. She remembers attending political meetings with her mother and her mother's woman friend in her childhood in the days before the vote. Although the women were interested it was the men of the village who were the central actors and arbitrators of political interests.

Even if the suffrage movement had been more aware of the radical changes that were needed to liberate women, had its members been more articulate about what might be the goals of a woman's party in working to establish a more equitable gender order and a more equitable division of labour, it seems probable that the very great divisions between the classes and the very real differences of class interests would have divided them. The nature of women's social position as wives and mothers meant that they did not have any organizations upon which to build. Unlike the other newcomers to the franchise, working-class men, women were therefore unable to develop a common set of organizations to provide a political base. The peculiarity of the social position of women was that their employers were also their husbands, lovers, the fathers of their children, men upon whom they were altogether dependent. In combining against the men each individual woman would be combining against the entirety of her life. Thus did the semi-feudal nature of the status of women defeat in some measure the individualistic freedom that had been so tardily won.

The growth of women's organizations

Political unity may not have been possible, but non-party political organization was. The constitutionalists of the old women's movement became the mothers of the National Union of Townswomen's Guilds. With over five million new women voters on the electoral register, as Stott (1978) recounts it developed a programme of 'comradeship, art and craft and citizenship'. While NUSEC continued to have a political programme, the NUTG concentrated on education, especially in 'home and family' issues with increasingly less emphasis on civics. Like its sister organization in rural areas, the Women's Institute, it provided a meeting place for thousands of women on the basis of one common denominator, as family members – and not as women in pursuit of equal rights. Mary Stott writes that in the 1930s it became obvious that,

> 'Henceforth, the older campaigning societies would shrink and the new social-cum-educational Guilds would burgeon. It was inevitable, for the major task of the suffrage societies had been completed and the supporters inevitably hived off into more specialized societies.' (Stott 1978 : 16)

Working through men inevitable

In a society where the public world had been exclusively controlled by men, the women had had to work through men to achieve the constitutional reforms; a revolution in which men were

88

rejected would have been the only other route, a route hardly practicable given the utter dependence of women on men in every social and economic sense. When they finally achieved the vote, therefore, defined primarily as wives and mothers, absent from positions of power in trade unions, capitalist industry, and the professions, having no organization and scant chance of developing any, women had neither the freedom nor the power to compete with men on equal terms in the public world.

The early women candidates

Women over thirty voted in the 'coupon' election of 1918 at the end of the First World War. Despite fears that women's entry into Parliament would lower the quality of debate and legislation, a bill had been passed to allow them to stand as candidates. Out of a total of 1,623 candidates, seventeen (just over 1 per cent) were women. The fears of Parliament, press, and public that Westminster would be submerged by a flood of women proved unfounded, as did the prophecy of some anti-suffragists that the more militant suffragists would be in the lead. In the sweeping victory for the coalition, Countess Markiewicz was the only successful woman. As a Sinn Fein candidate, she declined to take her seat at Westminster.

Of the seventeen pioneers in 1918, four stood as Labour, four as Liberal, and one as Conservative candidates, the remainder comprising six Independents and two Sinn Fein candidates. For the last two, women's rights and a place in the British Parliament were of secondary importance compared to Irish Home Rule. The high proportion of Independents undoubtedly reflects women's distance from the traditional male-dominated parties and their involvement in the suffrage campaign which meant that they were unable to rely on the electoral support of a party machine. Standing as a Women's Party candidate, Christabel Pankhurst was the only woman to get a coalition coupon. Independent women included Mrs Dacre Fox, an ex-militant suffragette, Emily Phipps, President of the National Federation of Women Teachers, Mrs Ray Strachey, a prominent member of the National Union of Women's Suffrage Societies. Three Labour candidates had also been active in the suffrage cause: Mrs Pethick Lawrence, Mrs Charlotte Despard, and Miss Mary Macarthur. The six Independents had little chance of success in a system predicated on party government. Apart from the successful Countess, only two women had any real electoral prospects: Christabel Pankhurst who lost by 775 votes and Mary Macarthur, who, having polled 7,587 votes, lost by 1,333.

The women, of course, had had no time to prepare for the 1918 election. Those in the three major parties had not been able to serve apprenticeships as candidates in unfavourable seats in order later to be selected for more favourable seats. It is not surprising therefore that there was no women's landslide and that neither the hopes of the suffragists nor the fears of the 'antis' were fulfilled.

In the five general elections during the next ten years, the number of women candidates increased slowly from seventeen in 1918 to sixty-nine in 1929 when women made up 4 per cent of all candidates. In the same period, the number of women MPs increased from one to fourteen, by which time they made up 2.3 per cent of all MPs. In that period the number of women standing as Independent candidates decreased. Women were absorbed into the male-dominated parties. This seems to reflect the liberal feminist consensus that women had achieved civil equality. The women pioneers were increasingly recruited from traditional party political backgrounds. The parties were predominantly organized around the disputes of men about control of resources in the public domain. Women were absent from positions of power within these parties and had difficulties in securing attractive candidacies. There was a general feeling in the Conservative Party that women were unsuitable parliamentary candidates. Mrs Baldwin, the Prime Minister's wife, stressed that the House of Commons was 'essentially a man's institution evolved through centuries by men to deal with men's affairs in a man's way' (quoted in Harrison 1978 : 234). As candidates, women in the Conservative Party were under-represented compared with the other two parties. Between 1918 and 1929 they comprised 1.3 per cent of all Conservative candidates at general elections compared to 3.5 per cent and 2.8 per cent in the Labour and Liberal parties respectively.

Preference for local government

Liddington and Norris suggest that many of the radical suffragists who had been involved in labour and suffrage campaigns preferred to stay close to their grass roots support and to work for the interests of women in their local community (1978 : 262). Many remained suspicious of the Labour Party's commitment to the interests of women and felt that women were not seen as equals within the movement: thus Hannah Mitchell 'was not prepared to be a camp follower, or a member of what seemed to be a permanent Social Committee, or official cake-maker to the Labour party' (1978 : 189). She preferred to work in local government with ILP support.

Women more easily saw a role that they could play in local government: it did not mean going so far away from home and could be fitted in well with a traditional female role. The increasing interest of the state in the family was to a large extent mediated through local government. The Women's Labour League realized the special contribution women could make:

'Women are needed badly for our *Municipal Housekeeping*.'

'Let us use our *women's brains and women's hearts* to help us guide the Labour policy on matters where we have knowledge and experience which men cannot have.'

'We women know the waste of precious time and health due to insanitary, crowded surroundings. Let us claim for ourselves and our children *decent homes to live in!*'

'Then we need to secure the appointment of well trained and properly paid *women sanitary inspectors*. They can visit in the homes and in the women's workrooms and shops, and give help and advice as no man inspector can do.' (quoted in Rendel 1977 : 58–9, emphasis in Rendel)

Women were also appointed to boards of guardians, education boards, and care committees, using every opportunity to persuade local authorities to make maximum use of their permissive powers in the interests of family welfare. During the First World War women's tasks expanded to include insurance, labour exchange, and distress committees. In all this activity women

91

emphasized the special nature of their contributions. In this way the different interests and capacities of women and men associated with the traditional division of labour in the family were carried over into the public world.

Marriage and family still dominant: the first women MPs

We saw in earlier chapters that in past history women had only occupied positions of power as a result of their membership of a particular family or their marriage to a man. The vote had given them the right to stand on their own behalf, as independent individuals. Given the millennia during which they had only ever exercised power or influence as surrogates for men, it should not perhaps surprise us that this is precisely the manner in which a number of the first women to enter Parliament achieved their seats; they were asked to do so by men in their families. Currell has clearly documented this process. Each of the first three women to enter the house were persuaded to do so by men and were expected to support the policies of their menfolk: Nancy Astor, Mrs Wintringham, and Mrs Mabel Hilton Philipson.

In 1919 the Conservative member for the Sutton Division of Plymouth was forced to give up a promising political career to go to the Lords following the death of his father, the first Viscount Astor. His wife, (Nancy) Lady Astor, was adopted as Conservative candidate in the subsequent by-election and became the first woman to sit at Westminster on 1 December, 1919. As the only woman among 600 men, everything she did was news and the practical issues of seating arrangements and the manner of address were the source of endless speculation. (Afterwards she maintained that she was so paralysed with fear that she sat through her first five hours in the House without movement.) But in all this excitement, as Pamela Brookes remarks, 'the irony of a situation in which an American-born woman was to be the first to sit in the British Parliament and moreover a woman who had never campaigned for women's political rights, was generally overlooked' (Brookes 1967 : 19).

The irony runs deeper. Nancy Astor had not sought a political position for herself, at least at the outset. She was standing as her husband's wife and not as a candidate in her own right. Furthermore as the quotation at the head of this chapter shows, it was her husband and not she who finally terminated her political career after the Second World War. Lady Astor not only used family resources but she acted very much in the traditional female mould: she worked in the interests of her husband. She was not reluctant to admit, even to exploit, the continuity in this relationship or her dependence on husband: ' "If you vote for me", she promised, "you will get tuppence for a penny, because you will be getting *me and my husband* as your representative. No other candidate can offer you as much. I belong to the tried old firm of Astor and Company" ' (quoted in Iremonger 1961 : 203, our emphasis).

These comments are not in any way to detract from the very real contribution she made in being the first woman to dilute ever so little the hitherto all-male club at Westminster. She made important debating contributions for many years and major contributions in her own right. The second woman member was also surrogate for a man. When the Liberal member for Louth died in 1921, his widow, Mrs Wintringham, was persuaded to fight the by-election. She sat in widow's weeds for most of the campaign, eminent liberals speaking on her behalf. In her short parliamentary career she spoke on a variety of topics including education, agriculture, and war pensions and like Lady Astor kept a watchful eye on measures affecting women and children. In 1922 she asked the Government for action to enable peeresses in their own right to sit in the House of Lords, thus initiating a campaign that was not resolved for another forty years. Lady Astor and Mrs Wintringham were joined the following year, after a by-election, by Mrs Mabel Hilton Philipson. She had also inherited her seat from her husband. He had been unseated as National Liberal member for Berwick on Tweed by petition and banned from standing for Parliament for seven years. Mrs Philipson agreed to stand, but as a Conservative, to keep his seat warm for him against his possible return. Her electoral success owed much to her husband's support throughout the campaign. In 1928 she stated her intention to retire since her husband no longer wished to return: 'the reason why I have held the seat had ceased to exist' (quoted in Brookes 1967 : 67). She wanted to pursue her own profession as an actress and to spend more time with her family.

In our view, the similarities between these three women are more important than their differences. They all were following in modified form the old tradition of women standing in for the men in their families. They were carrying over the relationship between husband and wife from the private domain into the public domain. This was a far cry from the individual rights of women.

Currell calls this type of activity, where a woman stands in for a man rather than standing in her own right, that is being a surrogate male, 'male equivalence' (Currell 1974 : 58). Currell suggests that this is more likely to be important in the early days following women's enfranchisement when the role of MP is a new one for women. She suggests that at such a time traditional behaviour may predominate. It does not seem to us that this need necessarily be the case, but given the failure of the feminist movement to address the question of the gender order and thus to prepare women better to act on their own, it probably was inevitable. The evidence for the period 1918 to 1929 supports Currell's (1974) hypothesis. During that period a total of thirteen women sat in the House of Commons, never more than ten at any one time: eight were married or widowed, and of these seven had replaced their husbands.

In addition to the three we have already discussed they included another three who were returned on their first attempt at by-elections: the Countess of Iveagh, returned to a safe Conservative seat inherited from her husband on his succession to the earldom, Mrs Walter Runciman, Liberal, and Mrs Hugh Dalton, Labour. In the last two cases the husbands were already in the House and both women were keeping more attractive seats warm for their husbands. Mrs Dalton, who sat for only a few months, provided a clear example of a woman acting entirely as a substitute for her husband. Without the advantages conferred on some women as a result of their relationships with a prominent man, women in this early period would not otherwise have achieved even these modest levels of representation. But family connections had other, no less significant results: many of these successful political women did not wish to enter the public world in their own right. The major impetus for them was their (wifely) desire or duty to promote the interests of their husbands. In this way, women's political interests were tied to those of men through the

94

peculiar nature of the marriage contract. No such bonds prevented the other late-comers to political rights, working-class men, from identifying and pursuing their own interests: the representatives of labour did not seek public office in order to promote the interests of employers.

While the idea that women in certain instances might act as substitutes for their men became less popular in later years, women continued to use resources deriving from their family positions to support their moves into the public domain. Family resources remained important for them since by and large they lacked other power bases in the worlds of industry, finance, and the professions. In this way family connections and reputation have been important for a minority of women who have attempted nonetheless to enter the world of politics in their own right to promote independent policies. Moreover for women from such families, the conventional division between the private and the public world, which impedes the entry of most women into the public domain, is less severe. For them, family backgrounds could be an advantage to be exploited. They are at least less constrained by the demands made on ordinary wives and mothers since they have access to some of their family's resources and can buy substitute care. Lady Astor undoubtedly benefited from the services of a large domestic staff at both Cliveden and the Astors' London house; she admitted that she could not have done so much without her three secretaries (Brookes 1967 : 27).

The independent women: individuals in their own right

It would be wrong to suppose that women were entirely reliant on their men or their families. Progress in entering the public domain was being made, albeit slowly. From 1919 women could no longer be disbarred from any profession and, although in a small minority, some women made headway in medicine and law. They remained organizationally weak for a long time. In the Civil Service there were new opportunities but women were not considered suitable candidates for certain posts and were expected to confine their attention to women and children.

Slow progress was made in the trade union movement also. By

1914 there were 437,000 women in trade unions out of a total membership of 4,145,000 (Mackie and Pattullo 1977 : 165). The problems of working women's dual role, assumptions about a woman's proper place, the nature of women's employment, as domestic servants or in small-scale enterprises including sweat-shops, all contributed. Women's isolation and potential for intimidation by employers was a major stumbling block to organization until the 1930s. When women were organized in mixed unions, their interests were thought of as secondary to those of men. Women-only unions did not have the strength to compete and to protect the interests of women when they conflicted with those of the men.

While women had replaced men in certain jobs during the First World War and had been able to explore new opportunities and to develop new skills, this 'dilution' was strongly resisted by the male craft unions. The women were expected to leave when men again became available. Women found it difficult to combine the demands of caring for a family with active involvement in union affairs. In their organizations working women relied heavily on help from middle-class women who more often had the time and the education to deal with their problems. The middle-class women in their turn relied on working-class women to relieve them of domestic chores.

Nevertheless some women were able to build a base in the trade union movement, even becoming national officials, though still largely confined to women's issues. It was from here that a minority including Susan Lawrence, Margaret Bondfield, and Ellen Wilkinson gained experience in public affairs and found support for their attempts to enter party and Parliamentary politics, usually in the interest of Labour.

It was in association with these other changes that were slowly beginning to take place in the wider society that not all the women who entered Parliament in the 1920s did so as surrogates for men or with bourgeois family support. A handful of women went into Parliament who were perhaps the portent of things to come.

Five new members were successful in the General Election of 1923, four of whom had won rather than inherited their seats. They included three Labour members who were heralded as a

96

new type of woman MP. All were single and had worked professionally in the trade union movement. Susan Lawrence, daughter of a solicitor and graduate of Newnham College, Cambridge, had been the first woman member of the London County Council in 1910. She had worked with Mary Macarthur in the National Federation of Women Workers. Margaret Bondfield entered Parliament at her third attempt. The daughter of a lace-maker, she started work as a shop assistant at the age of eleven. In 1899, as the only woman delegate to the TUC she spoke in support of the resolution which led to the creation of the Labour Party. She, too, had worked with Mary Macarthur and in 1923 was elected Chairman of the General Council of the TUC. The third member, Dorothy Jewson, came from a middle-class, professional family, was a graduate of Girton College, Cambridge, had also worked with Mary Macarthur and been an active suffragette. There was another Labour success in 1924. Ellen Wilkinson, born in Manchester, was the daughter of a cotton operative; she had won a scholarship to Manchester University, had been a trade union organizer, and was elected to Manchester City Council in 1923. These women were joined just before the 1929 General Election by Jenny Lee, the daughter of a Fifeshire miner, who at twenty-four became the youngest woman member of the House. A teacher, she had with the help of scholarships obtained a law degree from Edinburgh (Brookes 1967 : 66). The Labour women of the period 1918 to 1928 were distinguished from the other women MPs not only because they were all single at the time of their election, but because they had stood in their own right: they were not surrogate males. As Currell argues, they displayed a higher level of political motivation or commitment. While this is a difficult hypothesis to test, she offers 'various small pieces of evidence':

> 'It is clear from Margaret Bondfield's autobiography that her life was one of dedication to the furtherance of the Labour movement. Miss Wilkinson devoted her life to the Labour cause, as did Miss Susan Lawrence. An amusing sidelight comes from Earl Attlee's comment on the devotion of Miss Lawrence to the House of Commons. "I recall how exiled Susan Lawrence was when she lost her seat. 'Westminster, my

97

happy home, when shall I come to thee,' she would sing to me." ' (Currell 1974 : 59)

These levels of commitment to public office are clearly of a different order to that of Mrs Dalton, for example, whose interests were confined to the furtherance of her husband's political career.

Social origins of the women MPs

Because so few women were elected in this period, it is difficult to construct patterns from which to trace and compare more recent developments. But some tentative generalizations can be made. Considering the first eleven women MPs who sat between 1918 and 1928 (four Conservatives, four Labour, and three Liberals), and using such indicators as class origins and occupation, Currell (1974) suggests that the middle and upper classes were noticeably over-represented, although, as she says, this also applied to men MPs at that time. The Labour women MPs were rather different, since two of the four could be said to have been of working-class origin, even though they had been upwardly mobile through education and occupation. They were educationally distinctive:

'Three of the four in the Labour group were graduates, whereas none of the Conservatives and only one Liberal is known to have had a University education. This is, overall, a high proportion of graduates compared both with the general situation of higher education for women in this period, and with that of male MPs at that period.' (Currell 1974 : 56)

In summary, between the elections of 1918 and 1929, thirteen women had sat in the House of Commons, the record number of ten being reached just before the 1929 election (five Labour, four Conservative, and one Liberal). In all there had been fifteen successes in general elections out of a total of 125 candidatures.

Unity and disunity

The difficulties of united action by the women members and divisions about what their role should be were already apparent. There was no support for a Woman's Party. The Duchess of

98

Atholl, elected in 1923, had been opposed to women's suffrage and had spoken against Christabel Pankhurst's proposal for a Woman's Party. In her view a woman MP was elected by both sexes and she regretted women's 'charming habit of thinking that it is they who have sent you there and that you are only responsible to them' (quoted in Brookes 1967 : 51). Lady Astor was always welcoming to new women members of the House, but she thought a Woman's Party was impossible: 'We could not do it,' she said. 'We women disagree just as much as the men' (see Brookes 1967 : 25). Lady Astor had come in for a good deal of criticism from other women; for example, when she opposed a bill to reform the divorce law she had a heavy mail saying that she had no right to speak for women as a whole in this way (Brookes 1967 : 25). But there were examples of solidarity among the women: Mrs Philip Snowden refused an invitation to stand as a Labour candidate against Lady Astor, saying: 'I am a Labour woman, but the work which Lady Astor is doing for women and children both in Parliament and the country makes her services invaluable' (quoted in Brookes 1967 : 34).

But these were isolated examples. Like working-class men, women were new to the rights of political citizenship. Unlike the men they lacked organized bases from which to explore and exercise these newly acquired rights (see Currell 1974). The women's movement did not outlive the achievement of the vote, it had been united on that one demand; a woman's party did not emerge; no socialist feminist movement was consolidated and women did not achieve equality in the organizations of the Labour movement. Strachey, writing in 1928, saw the women's movement going forward 'as all the other movements for human progress will go forward, in the hands of the men and women of this generation' (Strachey 1978 : 392). From the women's point of view it was left to those exceptional women who could use their family resources or who, through individual mobility, particularly through education, could gain places in the professions or industry from which they could take political action. For the majority of women, whose primary responsibilities continued to be family-centred and whose only entry to the public world was likely to be to the world of work to improve the standard of life of their families, there were no such pathways to public power.

99

SIX

Women, power, and the family

'While occupancy of the traditional wife/mother/housewife constellation of roles . . . is correlated with certain types of powerlessness, it also has its own avenues of influence.' (Oakley 1974b : 14)

'The nuclear family (is a biological group) not a group based on a category of kin but on a class of inter-related activities. The weak link in this group is however the man.' (Harris 1969 : 67)

Introduction

As we saw in the last chapter, the first women to enter Parliament stood as surrogates for male members of their family, rather than as an assertion of their own individuality or because they had a specifically woman's point of view to forward. They had family sponsorship. We saw earlier that in some societies in the past and in some Islamic countries today, there was a strict division between the public world of men and the private world of women. We saw, however, that this did not mean that women were necessarily altogether powerless. Not only did they exert power in the private domain of the women, they were able to influence the decisions men took in the public domain because the men were connected to each other and to their husbands or sons. Women had this influence and power notwithstanding their profoundly inferior status. We also saw that women were involved in government where, as in Europe in Carolingian times, men held offices of state by virtue of their kin position and ruled from their family seats. When seats of government were set up separately from the dwelling place, women were excluded and lost power. At the same time, through marriage, liaisons, intrigue, in a later period through their *salons*, women continued to exert some influence although formally they were powerless. Any power that women had in the past, we concluded, came from their membership of family or kin groups and their social situation as daughters, wives, and mothers.

We concluded that it should not surprise us that the first women to enter Parliament did so from their position in the family. It should not surprise us since, for most women, this was the only base they had: they had no firm standing at all in the public world. The fight to enter the professions, to take part in government, to be accepted as persons, had been long and hard. The fight was against male-dominated institutions and with most men acting in concert to prevent women entering the public domain.

It has to be said that many women supported the men's opposition to the entry of women into the public world. They were the great majority of women who accepted the ideology that woman's proper place was in the home. Why did women continue to believe in this ideology? Were they just dupes of a dominant class of men, believing what men found it convenient for them to believe? Or was the place that women had within the private domain one in which they received certain rewards, social as well as material? Is this still the case? Is this why women are still in a minority in the public domain? Do they have benefits

101

and power in the private domain which they value? Are women, as some men argue, so comfortably placed at home that they have more to lose than to gain if they 'go out', whether to work or to enter politics? And even if this implies far too cosy a view of what it is to be a housewife and mother (as most women would agree (Oakley 1974b)), is it that the traditional wife-mother role has satisfactions which outweigh those that it is possible to gain in the public world? Or are women just trapped in the family?

In order to try and answer these questions we will look at the empirical evidence about what goes on in the nuclear family. Who has the power? What power? Is there a private domain for women in twentieth-century Britain? In answering these questions we shall try to take account of the social and political economy of the societies in which the families are located. It would be quite incorrect to look at these micro-politics of the families as if there was free rein for the couple to come to whatever decision they wished as to who did what and who wielded power or exercised authority inside the family, in its day-to-day arrangements and in the rearing of the children. In advanced industrial societies of complex social structure, regional variation, and elaborated historical development, one can reasonably expect to find variations. At the same time, such variations have not occurred randomly. Each couple in setting up home, in establishing a way of life, is constrained by various exterior factors: the economy, the laws, the norms of the majority. In addition there is the possibility of individual families living by the scarcely changed ideologies of an earlier period, a sort of 'cultural lag' in Ogburn's sense, or copying what they believe to be the values and behaviour of a reference group, a group to whom they refer for ideas and standards about how to live.

As we said in the Introduction, when we speak of power we not only mean those circumstances in which the will of one person triumphs over that of another; we also mean those circumstances in which the views, interests or wishes of one category or group are normally given precedence, in which there is not struggle or conflict, but in which their superiority is taken for granted either because that is believed to be correct or because there appears to the subordinate persons no way to make a challenge. Power that is wielded without challenge, so that it hardly appears that one is imposing his (sic) will on another is particularly likely to occur in male-female relations (cf.Bell and Newby 1976). So many of the issues that concern women are not on the public agenda, are not seen as matters which are in dispute, are not seen as power issues at all.

This has to be borne in mind when we look at the evidence of field data, for the taken-for-granted may well be taken for granted by the field workers too and may therefore not get the research attention that it should. This is clear in a number of the studies we shall look at where a particular division of labour between the sexes within the nuclear family was taken for granted. Thus Elizabeth Bott reports that in all her families, although they varied a great deal in their social arrangements, there was a basic division of labour,

> 'by which the husband was primarily responsible for support-
> ing the family financially and the wife was primarily respons-
> ible for housework and child care; each partner made his [sic]
> own differentiated but complementary contribution to the
> welfare of the family as a whole.' (Bott 1968 : 54)

Similar statements about this fundamental gender order are made for Gosforth (Williams 1956 : 41), Westrigg (Littlejohn 1963 : 122), Banbury (Stacey 1960 : 136), St Ebbes (Mogey 1956 : 55). In Banbury and in St Ebbes the distinction is also made about certain 'dirty' or 'heavy' tasks which it is thought appropriate for men to do (no mention being made of other dirty and heavy tasks that it was appropriate for women to do, like washing dozens of dirty nappies and other soiled linen by hand, cf. Whitehead 1976). It was not until the 1970s, when Oakley studied housewives, that a researcher overtly questioned the rightness of this gender order and systematically asked women what they thought about it. In the seventies, too, Frankenberg (1976) discussed his field data from Pentrediwaith (1957) and showed that formerly he had accepted without question certain facets of the gender order. Although his intention had been to analyse and describe a society where the total dependence of women was made incomplete by the partial inability of men to earn a living, he now argues that he made inadequate use of his case data. While he still thinks he was right that the women dominated the social life of the village he did not comment on 'the lack of women as officials of village societies despite their informal leadership and', he adds, 'I might have provided a more convincing analysis of both this and the defeat of the women's parish council candidate' (Frankenberg 1976 : 36).

Much writing on the family assumes that a 'democratic, egalitarian family', within which the sexes are equal, has emerged during the twentieth century. Blood and Wolfe's (1960) study of power relations between husbands and wives in 1955 is an example of this stance. The study has been extensively criticized, notably by Safilios-Rothschild (1969) and Gillespie (1971). Blood and Wolfe's analysis has an old-fashioned ring when read twenty years later with benefit of the writing and thinking of the new feminist movement. Blood and Wolfe's evidence shows some variation from one couple to another and some systematic variation among families. What is most clear, however, from the variables they used to measure the power relation, is that women neither have a private domain of their own, nor do they have equality of decision-making in matters that gravely affect their lives, nor do they have the same freedom as men to enter the public domain. Despite this, Blood and Wolfe conclude that 'the predominance of the male has been so thoroughly undermined that [they] no longer live in a patriarchal system' (1960 : 19).

Perhaps one can understand that men might have felt that changes in the relative power of the sexes had gone further in the 1950s than later research suggests. But it is clear that Blood and Wolfe had no very radical changes in mind. They share with their sample the assumption that women not only bear but should also rear children and that women's activities must be constrained thereby. Furthermore, in any partnership where this division of labour in the family does not apply, where the woman is the more powerful and the regular breadwinner, they consistently speak of the male partner as having 'failed', being 'inadequate' or 'indecisive'. This value-judgement is complementary to that of Klein and the authors she quotes who describe mothers in families where women are dominant as 'overprotective' (Klein 1965).

In addition to this difficulty in distancing oneself from one's own society that all social investigators experience, there are particular problems about discovering who wields what power and how much power they wield in the family (cf. Bott 1968 : 22; Safilios-Rothschild 1970 : 549). Furthermore, we disagree with Safilios-Rothschild who appears to believe that it is possible to understand power in the family without seeing that family as part of a wider society. Therefore, we have looked at a number of studies that have set the family in its social context, as well as drawing upon others where we know something of the socio-economic and politico-legal background of the society in question. The overall conclusion that we have come to after examining this evidence accords with the view held by Goode (1963) and Gillespie (1972) that what has been called the 'demo-cratic, egalitarian family' has reduced the autonomy of women in the domestic sphere and has removed or reduced any private domain that there might once have been. Furthermore, while in one sense upper-class women and to some extent middle-class women were and are clearly advantaged in relation to working-class women, some middle-class women are at least as subordi-nated to their men (and their men's work) as are working-class women. It is too simple just to say that working-class women suffer a double oppression. It is true they suffer the oppression of the working class and the oppression of women, but some middle-class women, wives of capitalist farmers and wives of corporate managers, suffer a special oppression. We will examine the evidence for these propositions. Our concern is not only with the relative power relations between men and women but also between parents, especially women, and children.

Joint and segregated conjugal role relations

Elizabeth Bott was among the first to look at the internal dynam-ics of the family and it is possible to relate what she has to say to our notions of a public and a private domain. In studying her twenty London families Bott distinguished those couples who had a segregated role relationship, i.e. in effect led separate lives side by side, from those who had joint conjugal role relations, i.e. who shared activities, friends, and social life. In the first case there was a clearly defined division of labour between husband and wife. This went along with the wife being embedded in a close-knit network of social relations composed of her female kin and her female neighbours, something akin to a private domain. The men also had their separate network. The men were said to be authoritarian and the families mother-centred. There is, as Bott points out, no contradiction here for each partner has authority in her/his own field (Bott 1968 : 64).

This comment of Bott's is central to the thesis of this book, although the terminology is different. What she is referring to is a private domain of the woman in which she has power and authority. It seems possible, given what Bott says about the nature of the close-knit networks, the way they overlap, and the power of gossip, that the women in these families may be not altogether powerless to influence the men indirectly, although this could only be the case where the separate networks of husband and wife overlapped. In so far as they are quite distinct, there is no way in which the women could bring any influence to bear upon the men. The women might be mutually supportive of each other, but their structural positions would not give them the kinds of power that we saw Muslim women, for example, could wield. Those couples who had a joint conjugal role relationship had a more flexible division of labour and joint consultation on all major decisions. This was within the basic and universal division between child-rearer-and-housewife versus breadwinner, a division that was not questioned in any of Bott's families. We cannot help wondering how the 'democracy' worked out in practice. It is clear that the wives found their position in these families difficult: 'They complained of isolation, boredom and fatigue. They wanted a career or some special interest that would make them feel that they were something more than children's nurses and housemaids' (1968 : 83). For them, there was no private domain, but no place in the public domain either.

Catholic mothers in country and town

There have been societies in the Western world in recent times in which there were clearly distinguished private worlds of women and a public world of men. One such was the rural society of County Clare in Ireland in the 1930s, described by Arensberg and Kimball (1940). They report a society deeply segregated by sex in which the women were undoubtedly in a subordinate position,

106

their role was one of service, although it included hard tasks.

The wife was responsible for day-to-day housekeeping and the care of the children. She waited on the menfolk at table, not eating until they were finished. She had various farm tasks to do, such as milking and feeding animals. In the evening when, at slacker times of the farm year, the men rested, she continued working, helping the children, knitting, and baking and it was she who closed the house for the night, having been the first to rise and start the fire.

There were critical times of the year when all the family were needed in the fields, turf making, hay making, potato planting. All family members had clearly allocated tasks and worked under the direction of the farm owner who was also husband and father. He could order the male tasks as he saw fit yet his first charge was to the family he headed (Arensberg and Kimball 1968 : 46). 'While he may demand and expect of his wife that she fulfil her household duties, so may she demand and expect that he fulfil his in the management and working of the farm and in providing for herself and the children' (Arensberg and Kimball 1968 : 47). Arensberg and Kimball stress the complementarity and the reciprocity in this relationship. The division of labour they saw as rooted in 'nature'.

But the women were not altogether without power over men, for their sons were subordinate to them; only in cases of grave indiscipline was the father's authority sought. 'In the farm work the boy is subject to commands of his mother even when, fully adult, he has passed over exclusively to men's work' (Arensberg and Kimball 1968 : 57).

Irishmen in that society were 'boys', even though middle-aged, until they had inherited or taken over a farm to run themselves. Thus widows could command sons to run farms. At the same time, from the earliest days a close affectual relationship developed between mothers and sons, the young son being by his mother's side throughout her working day in the house and outside around the farmyard.

While the 'boy' ultimately became a man in command of his own farm, no such transformation awaited the daughter. When she married she not only continued to serve the men, she also became subservient to her husband's mother away from her natal home on her mother-in-law's territory. This was so because the society was not only patriarchal and patrilineal, but also patri-local, that is the wife was brought into the husband's family and took his surname (patronym). Marriages were typically arranged by marriage brokers. Individual choice was accorded to neither partner.

Did the segregated role relationships, the separation of the men's domain from the women's domain render the women powerless or powerful? Did the women form groups which could bring influence to bear upon the men? Arensberg and Kimball were both men and, as we have seen earlier, their data and interpretation is likely to express a male view of the world. Yet it seems doubtful that there was a unity among the women, for the mother-in-law/daughter-in-law relationship was full of tension and conflict.

There were gatherings of men, of young men and of old men, wherein the traditions of the society were passed on and through which social control was exercised, as well as recreation taken. The last days of the elderly were passed in company of those of the same sex. The women did not have similar groups: their relationships with other women appear to have been confined to the house and the kin. We do not know, because it is not a subject of focus for Arensberg and Kimball, how much in practice the women could influence the outcome of events either in the life of the family and the farm, or of the wider community. Certain it is that they had their sphere, that it was a subordinate sphere to that of the men but that with regard to that sphere the men would defer to the women as experts. Women seem to have been subservient but not totally oppressed. A woman's main task was clearly to conceive, suckle, and rear children. The more she successfully produced, the higher was the esteem in which she was held. Along with the tasks of household and farm this cannot have left the County Clare women much time or energy for the manipulation of public affairs. But they did have a domain which was in many senses their own.

In Chapter 2 we saw how the cult of Marianism within the Catholic Church was associated with according considerable amounts of power and authority to women and especially to the mothers of families. This was so despite an ideology and social

108

institutions which gave women a secondary place to men and excluded them from the public domain.

Josephine Klein, in her impressive survey *Samples from English Cultures*, concludes that in the 'traditional working class', while most of the North of England 'is markedly male-dominant in power and privilege', where 'the Irish have spread from Liverpool, the mother seems to hold sway' (1965 : 176).

Mays's (1954) reports of Liverpool's dockland describe a male-dominated family pattern, but in the Catholic families of Ship Street studied by Madeleine Kerr (1958) the husband-father cuts very little ice (Klein 1965), having little authority in the family. The only respectable role for a man in Ship Street was to conform to the wishes first of his mother and then of his wife. While husbands in County Clare would in the end side with their wives against their mothers, the Ship Street men sided with their mothers against their wives. The women had a domain which was shared by women of older and younger generations, daughters frequently living with their mothers, bringing their husbands with them, willing to leave the men behind if they did not wish to come. Wives in County Clare lived with their mothers-in-law; in Ship Street they lived with their own mothers. This appears to have increased their solidarity as women but not increased the loyalty of their husbands to them. But as some of them told Kerr, they felt they could manage quite well without their husbands but could not manage without their mothers.

Men are seen as inferior to women in the sense, as Klein puts it, that,

> 'one gains the impression that whereas the daughter interacts with her mother on a footing of potential equality – being regarded as an apprentice "Mum" – the son interacts with his mother on an unequal footing, always subordinate since he cannot by reason of his sex ever hope to perform her role.' (1965 : 56)

Kerr did not discuss the man's world of work; what we know of this has to be gleaned from the Liverpool study of dockland. We do know something of the work done by the husbands in Kerr's study. About a quarter were sailors, a third were dockers (although some men may have alternated between these two tasks) and about a quarter were in casual, unskilled labour, unemployed or in jail. The dominant position taken by the women may therefore be partly explained by the men being absent from home a good deal of the time. But this cannot be the whole explanation, for many of the men were in regular work and at home.

In the case of County Clare there is a clear ideology of complementarity, of segregated roles in which women are expected to marry, to bear and rear children, and to serve their men. In exchange for this service the mother is idealized at the same time as she is constrained, although she does have limited freedom and power. The ideology is reinforced by the theory and practice of the Church. How suffocating some women may find this allotted place has been sensitively expressed by Edna O'Brien, especially in her earlier novels, and in *Mother Ireland*, 'the family tie that is more umbilical than among any other race on earth. The martyred Irish mother' (O'Brien 1978 : 19). Migrated from the unitary society and settled in an industrial town where the social networks are different, and the men are not farmers but employees at the mercy of their masters and the economy, the authority of the Irish mother in the home appears to be more complete. Her work is nevertheless hard and unremitting and her material resources slender. When Barbara Harrell-Bond (1969) interviewed couples on a new housing estate in Oxford, she found that husbands from Southern Ireland developed a network of Irish friends with whom they spent a great deal of time. This their wives did not do, probably because their housewifely role tied them to the estate and they lacked Irish neighbours. The Irish pattern of a clearly distinct division of labour persisted. These Irish women, therefore, seem still to have their domain but lack supporting female friends or kin. Harrell-Bond concludes: 'It was my impression that generally Irish women expressed feelings of dissatisfaction and unhappiness which apparently their husbands did not share' (1969 : 87).

Complementarity or conflict?

In the predominantly Protestant rural area of Gosforth in what we now call Cumbria, 'there is a fairly clear division of labour

110

between the sexes' (Williams 1956 : 41), but the women do not appear to be so idealized and the sexual divisions are perhaps not quite so strictly marked. Relationships are again symbolized by seating arrangements at meal times, but if commensality (eating together) is a sign of greater equality, then Gosforth women are less subservient than the women of County Clare. 'At the table the occupier (who may be owner or tenant farmer) sits at one end and his wife at the other. The occupier's children sit at his end of the table . . . and the farm servants at the wife's end' (Williams 1956 : 35).

Whatever may be the symbolism of having servants sit near the wife (relegation to the lower end beneath the children, or for the servants to be under the wife's eye?), the division of labour, while clear, does not seem to imply total subordination for the wife. Generally women's work is confined to the house and near it. They care for house, children, pigs, and poultry and the money they earn from the latter activities is theirs to use as they wish, as was also the case in County Clare. The men do not know how much 'pin money' their women make. However, the wives do not use this 'pin money' on themselves, but for maintaining the farm-house and for clothes for the adult women. According to Williams, 'The wife is therefore largely independent, and may indeed have inherited sums of money from her parents . . . so that she may be more wealthy than her husband' (1956 : 41). But there is more to it than that:

> 'on a great many farms the farmer's wife handles all the money and it was common to hear her referred to jocularly as "t'Chancellor of the Exchequer" . . . . In some families separate accounts are kept, but as a rule the wife handles all the bills and money, while the farmer signs the cheques and visits the bank.' (1956 : 42)

William goes on to say that the farmers considered the wife's dominance [sic] in financial matters as a threat to their position as head of the household' (1956 : 42).

Williams had no woman research associate, although doubtless he had help from among the female population, so we have no direct accounts by women, given to a woman, of how they felt about this matter. In the private domain it would seem that

111

women could clearly exercise a good deal of influence if they had a mind to. But note that the ultimate control of the bank account remained with the man, in whose name it was, and it was the men who took any necessary action in the public domain, doing the business at the bank itself. This men did not delegate. Does this imply female 'dominance' (see Hunt 1978b)?

While widows could inherit from their husbands and live on the holding, many wills had 'special clauses designed to ensure that the widow [did] not change the succession favoured by her husband' (Williams 1956 : 52). In inheritance there was a preference for the eldest son. As to the propertyless villagers, we learn that 'In many families where the parents are young, the house-wife's position is much less subordinate than that of the farmer's wife' (Williams 1965 : 58).

In Williams's account, as in the account of County Clare, there is the underlying notion of complementarity between the sexes without hint of struggle or antagonism. Frankenberg discerned conflict between the sexes in Pentrediwaith (1957) as we have seen. Whitehead saw it as an important organizing principle in the Herefordshire village she studied in the 1960s. Not only did she find that the worlds of women and men were segregated, they were also *opposed*. Marriage was morally right, it was 'the normal and ideal state for adults' (Whitehead 1976 : 183). Cross gender contact only occurred sufficiently for courtship to come about, boys and men continuing to go out together, just reserving certain nights for courting, 'but once married they did not even reserve Friday and Saturday for their wives' (Whitehead 1976 : 175; see also Dennis, Henriques, and Slaughter 1974). The marriage partnership was markedly asymmetrical. There was almost complete absence of wage work for women, so they were financially dependent on their husbands who gave them a fixed amount of money. The men did not hand over their pay packet and women might not know how much their husbands earned. There was a clear division of labour accepted by women as well as men: the husband the breadwinner and the wife the house worker. When the wives went to hospital other women, usually relatives, looked after their husbands.

Marriages were generally stable, but at the same time in many there was socially visible quarrelling, especially in the child

112

rearing years: spouses locked each other out of the house, refused to perform their respective domestic chores, had physical fights (see Brown and Harris (1978) on the withdrawal of the husband from the wife in the child-rearing years). Despite this, women complained when their husbands went out to the pub too much. 'The desire for more of a husband's company is not a contradiction of the segregated division of labour. You do not have to conceive of a husband as a friend, or similar to youself, in order to want him in the house. What is wanted perhaps is the sense that your work in the house is valued' (Whitehead 1976 : 189). The antagonism between the sexes was not only found within the family. It emerged in the social exchanges in the pub in which there was a great deal of mockery and teasing, much of it obscene and sometimes brutal. The major point of some of this teasing was about how well a man could control his wife, about which of the partners was in control. The joking was competitive and a man who was known to have been locked out would lose in the banter. Much of the pub joking was designed to maintain a particular and subordinate gender definition of women.

While related women did help each other, were mutually supportive, and took some recreation together, Whitehead does not believe that the female kin provided a solidary group in which women helped each other against their husbands. Mothers, in particular, did not support their daughters. 'The major basis for women's solidarity (the kin group) turned out to entrench them further in deference, powerlessness, and in many cases, personal misery' (Whitehead 1976 : 198). Whitehead formed the impression that women kin members, the 'women's trade union', is less solidary than had elsewhere been reported by several ethnographers, for example, Stacey (1960). Perhaps too much was made of that point. It would not have been true that mothers in Banbury around 1950 did not try to encourage their daughters to 'make a go' of their marriages, it was much more that in the absence of any other solidary group and in the isolated position of wife-mother, women had no other place to turn if their marriage became intolerable. This would appear to be the Herefordshire situation also, except that in Banbury in 1950 as in Swansea in 1960 (Stacey 1960, 1965) if 'push came to shove' mothers would take their daughters in rather than see them in the street. The

113

more powerless a woman in the household, however, the less might she be able to do this. In Banbury there were many variations around the norm, given the diverse origins of the inhabitants, the class and religious differences among them.

In the fifties in Ashton, the Northern mining town (Dennis, Henriques, and Slaughter 1974) one has the clear impression of a sex-segregated, male-dominated society with considerable antagonism between the sexes. The man's world of the mine and the club and the woman's world of the home were clearly separate, wives being expected to provide defined services for their husbands. A meal should not only be ready when he came home, but be prepared from raw ingredients. Shop substitutes were rejected and thrown on the back of the fire. This was also the destination of women's contraceptives, acquired by a few brave women in an attempt to control their fertility. The transition from a boy, largely under female supervision, to a man under male surveillance in a man's world was clearly marked. When the boys went down the mine they became men and were taught to swear as men swear. This was the men's world from which women were excluded. But the women were not quite without power, albeit a supernatural power, as we discussed in Chapter 2 (p.21–2). There we suggested that perhaps men, having oppressed women, are fearful of their restlessness, their possible uprising or, more sinister because invisible, the exercise of their supernatural powers against men. In an industry like coal mining where there are daily and unknown hazards and in the situation of oppression which the men themselves are in, such fear of the supernatural would not be altogether surprising.

Women's subordination and social class

Many studies give a strong impression of marked class differences. It is clear that the material standard of life of middle-class and upper-class women is a great deal more comfortable than that of the working class: housing is more generous, food is more available, there is less pinching and scraping to be done. Working-class families suffer all manner of oppressions not felt, or not felt so often or to the same degree, by middle-class families. In the

middle and upper classes life is more predictable, more comfortable, and sometimes more elegant. It is not certain, however,
that in terms of their relative oppression by men, working-class
women are always worse off. Certainly they suffer a double
oppression, but some middle-class women are extremely constrained by their husbands and their husbands' work situation as
we shall see. This may emerge in long-term life chances rather
than in day-to-day matters. And Oakley found no clear class
differences in women's attitude to and experience of housework
(Oakley 1974a) or mothering, although working-class women
appeared to be more accepting of the housework they had to do
than the middle class (cf. Rosser and Harris (1965 : 208–09) who
report working-class wives to be more domesticated).

For Westrigg, in the Cheviot Hills, Littlejohn described a status
for the wife in the household which improves the higher up the
social scale one goes. This was symbolized by mealtime arrangements. In the upper class everyone, including the wife, sat down
at the table together. While she served them, she was in command of the situation and the entire meal was surrounded by
much ceremony all of which 'emphasizes the control the housewife has over food. One gets food by virtue of her kindness'
(Littlejohn 1963 : 128). In the working class the arrangements
and behaviour were different. The wife might well walk round
pouring everyone's tea before sitting down herself; milk, sugar,
and food were all in the centre of the table and reached for by
whoever wanted it 'the wife here has no control over the food but
instead performs a servantlike role during the meal' (Littlejohn
1963 : 129).

The women themselves were divided by class: there was no
cross-class visiting. Middle-class women 'stand in a relation of
patronage to working-class women' (Littlejohn 1963 : 131). The
use of the male term 'patronage' is probably correct in this context, since the middle-class women's ability to dominate the
working-class women derived from the respective positions of
their husbands in the economic system. But, Littlejohn argues,
there was nothing to bring women into opposition with each
other as the employer-employee relationship brought the men
into opposition. The women might not have been united but the
men certainly were divided. At the same time women played a

115

part in the maintenance of the class system. While in the working class the wife could 'have no responsibility for gaining status for her family but she (had) a great deal of responsibility for maintaining its status and (could) be responsible for its downfall into a non-respectable "slum class" ' (Littlejohn 1963 : 123). This is a circumscribed and negative role. Littlejohn adduces evidence to show that 'the higher the class the less dominant the male and the less distance between the sexes' (Littlejohn 1963 : 126). Or is the male domination just more subtle and discreet? According to Littlejohn, in the working class except for dancing and courtship, there were distinct male and female domains, while recreational activities were shared in the middle classes. Working-class women rarely drove cars; lower-middle-class women did but were less skilled than their men; most upper-middle-class women drove and were as skilled as their men. Working-class husbands sometimes censured wives in front of their children, the women had to take a back seat when visitors were present or join in on male topics. Chivalry was exhibited in the middle class where women may initiate conversation even about women's topics (e.g. children) and the men would join in but women could also initiate topics, like politics, which relate to the public domain of men. Although the women were dealt with more discreetly, did not the very ceremonies, like opening doors for them, define their subordinate place?

In Gosforth it seemed that property-owning led the farmers to keep a tighter rein on their wives than the village workers did. It is clear that economic circumstances may make important variations, although, as we have seen, they may be cross-cut by religion. The households were dominated by women in Branch Street, a deprived inner city area which Paneth (1944) got to know when she went there as a war-time social worker and which was also later studied by Spinley (1954). The men were mostly unskilled and lowly paid, unemployed or in casual employment. The man was regarded as the official head of the household, but he was seldom home to exercise his authority over his wife (or woman) or the children. Often this 'head' was a succession of the mother's male partners. The women were expected not only to bear but also, as everywhere, to rear the children, and they were also expected to take waged work except when the

116

children were young. Male domination was asserted through the sexual act in an aggressive manner. Paradoxically all the girls wanted to marry and initiated courtship, although one at least had been so put off by witnessing her mother's experiences during sex and the violence of the man, that she had vowed not to marry. While there was marked sex segregation, no private domain for the women was possible in the house because of the severely cramped living conditions.

The Branch Street men fell among those whom Blood and Wolfe would call 'failures'. But how can one use such a phrase when the pattern of mother-headed households is the norm for the district? Blood and Wolfe's Detroit study led them to conclude that 'working-class families tend to be more wife-dominated in their power structure' than middle-class families (1960 : 34). Black working-class wives took the greatest responsibility of all for earning and making decisions in their families. But it is important to note that these were also the wives who worked more than forty hours a week outside the home and who also got the least help from their husbands of any group of working-class wives. Blood and Wolfe find it paradoxical that these 'powerful wives' did not compel their husbands to do more work. What a misunderstanding! These wives make the household decisions because their husbands leave it to them. There was nothing in those decisions that could be of material importance to the men, so they did not bother. But the surrounding world was male-dominated and in it men did not do housework. The poorest wives, therefore, were left with the most work and almost sole responsibility. They were in charge of what there was to be in charge of, but that was not much.

Blood and Wolfe's data suggest that the higher the status of the husband, the greater was his power in the home. In particular, high status husbands made more decisions in the three areas of whether to buy life insurance, what house or apartment to get, and especially whether the wife should take or leave a job. High status husbands were more apt to handle the money and the bills. This Blood and Wolfe argue, no doubt correctly, was because in families with high status husbands 'there is a larger increment of money involved beyond the level of daily necessities' (1960 : 33). The house and the insurance are investment matters; high status husbands are not worried about loss of prestige if their wives work, but they are concerned about the problems involved: 'the reorganization of *their* family life around a working wife' (1960 : 33, our emphasis). Blood and Wolfe read this male dominance as the more active sharing of responsibility by high status husbands compared with low status husbands whom they saw as 'failing' to take part in the decision-making process. Blood and Wolfe are in the end aware that they are not comparing like with like across the classes. Decisions about insurance and houses are quite different decisions for the rich and the poor. It is only executives who want to keep their wives at home to act as hostesses. The poor whites and even more the poor blacks may leave decisions to their wives. When property was involved, however, there was at best benevolent repression, the husbands not only controlling their own and their wives' jobs, and the car, but the family finances as well. These data hardly suggest the end of 'patriarchy' which Blood and Wolfe claimed had already come about.

More recent data collected for Britain by Jan and Ray Pahl (1971) suggest that the relationship of managers to corporate capitalism has repressive consequences for their wives. This is a matter which is also discussed by Dorothy Smith (1974). The Pahls' managers' wives were for the most part at home with their children. Only thirteen out of eighty-six were working full- or part-time. When those who intended to take a job later were added the proportion was slightly less than half. All of the women were agreed that their husbands' jobs came first. This, associated with the geographical mobility of managers, made it extremely difficult for the women to follow any career. Furthermore, 'For several, the heavy demand of their husband's work meant they were responsible for more of the household chores than are wives of junior white collar workers . . . whose husband might be free to spend evenings and weekends on joint activity around the home' (Pahl and Pahl 1971 : 120). Some wives reported being depressed and many had identity problems.

The Pahls sum the situation up thus:

'If being a housewife were defined as "work" and as "a job" then perhaps a choice could more easily be made. But some

118

how a different, more emotive value is put on being a house-wife, which also affects the value of any job she does. The housewife role is not thought to be greatly esteemed by society, but she is expected to be totally committed to it. A housewife – as most of the women in our study took for granted – is expected to subordinate her own interests to the interests of her husband, children and home.' (1971 : 138)

But despite their managerial position, these husbands were also subordinated. They were subordinated to the firms for which they worked. When they were told that they had to move to another post, most probably in another part of the country, they simply accepted it. It was not a matter for discussion with their wives: it was not a matter for discussion *at all*. The managers and their wives only felt they had control in the domestic sphere, over the education of their children and the influence they could bring to bear on their children's future careers.

The Pahls compare their couples with the graduate couples studied by Fogarty, Rapoport, and Rapoport (1971b). The gradu-ate couples both shared a high degree of commitment to their work and attempted to solve the woman's 'dual career' problems on an egalitarian basis. Bott (1968) discusses the complexity of the relationships when wives work and refers to Rapoport and Rapoport (1969) who suggest that where both partners work they may develop much more distinct domains. The relationships do not seem to be just a matter of middle-classness but having to do with the structure of corporate capitalism and the relationship of the couple to corporate capitalism.

This Dorothy Smith has explored in some depth. In her view it is not the division of labour between the sexes, as such, which leads to the oppression of women by men, it is 'the constitution of public versus private spheres of action, and the relegation of the domestic to that sphere which is outside history' (Smith 1974 : 7). The development of corporate capitalism has changed the relationship of the manager to the mode of production, has transformed the relationship of the bourgeoisie to the productive enterprise. It has subordinated managers to the corporation. Smith argues that while the manual worker suffers alienation of her/his product, in the case of the manager or technical specialist it is the *act* that is appropriated and it is the *person* that is alienated. In contrast to the Pahls, whose work is largely descriptive and who are concerned solely with the micro-politics of husband-wife relations in the home, Smith seeks to link the macro-structure to the political economy of the family. Thus she argues that the alienation of the worker under capitalism has the effect of transforming the work of women into a personal service, private and outside history. This is true for both working- and middle-class women. Managers are men and their wives are assigned to the home. But there is a crucial difference because the middle-class family stands in a sub-contractual relation to corporate capitalism in a way in which the working-class does not. Sally in Oakley's (1974a) study shares the same view: Sally said the husband-wife relationship is like boss and worker. Or in Smith's words: 'The underlying determinants of the relation between men and women is this relation to the economic structure whereby the relation of wife to husband mimics the relation of husband to capitalist' (1974 : 6). This was a point made strongly for the miners by Dennis, Henriques, and Slaughter (1974). The Pahls' middle-class respondents also make it plain. The security of the managers' wives depends on their husbands. Their husbands' security depends on their jobs, i.e. their bosses.

The relation of the middle-class family to corporate capitalism becomes analogous to the working-class family, but the middle class, although separated now from ownership of the means of production, are nevertheless part of the ruling class of the bourgeoisie. Thus responsibility for the maintenance of the moral order falls upon them. The middle-class family is 'sub-contracted' to corporate capitalism, the family has to do what must be done for the members of the corporation and to keep the image of the corporation and its appropriate moral order intact. This is the women's task. Smith argues that the working-class family is privatized and women in it do not have this same responsibility. This begs the question of the working-class woman's responsibility for the reproduction of the labour force. Nor does it allow for the working-class wife any responsibility for the reproduction of the class system. Littlejohn (1963) pointed to the role of all women in this (see p. 115–16 above). Women of all classes would seem to be involved in the reproduction of class relations, including their own oppression in that system. Smith's point is close to Littlejohn's and also goes further. It relates to the consumption-dominated society which has burgeoned in greater force since Littlejohn was writing in the sixties. 'The activity of the man translated into money and the labour of the woman in the home, pass over into display rather than an exchange of benefits as the mode in which their activity is brought into relation with others (Smith 1974 : 22). Instead of a 'working order' the media present a 'display order', an order which expresses the moral and financial status of the household. The middle-class woman is mainly responsible for presenting the image of this moral order but at the same time her work is trivialized. Furthermore, what she is doing, she is doing as the agent of the external order, an order imposed by corporate capitalism and appropriated by men. There is a great deal in Smith's argument but we feel that working-class women (except the very poorest) are also unwittingly recruited as agents of corporate capitalism: through their role as the family shoppers they are a major means whereby the market is manipulated. In our view this can arguably be interpreted as against the interests both of their class and their sex.

It seems clear to us that despite the variations in family formation and the relationships between the partners which were found by both Oakley (1974a, 1974b) and the Pahls, the kinds of relationships that emerge are not simply a matter of micro-politics dependent on the attitudes of the partners. This is what the Pahls imply, both in their comparison with the 'dual career' families and in their conclusion about future change. Here they speculate that in future wives may be less docile and also that husbands may be less prepared to accept the orders of higher management, both because their wives will not put up with it, but also because they themselves may be expected to be less biddable. How biddable any of us is must depend greatly on economic and political factors outside individual control. With high inflation rates increasing numbers of husbands are grateful for the earnings their wives may bring in; in times of recession it may be a question of doing what the company says or losing your job. Public expenditure cuts by governments responsive to the wishes of international capitalists may alter entire career patterns. Certainly generational changes can and do occur, but the

121

present evidence suggests that the relationship between the family form and the employment situation is strong.

No private domain but an equal partnership?

In some twentieth-century societies and some parts of those societies we have located a private domain of the women; we have also found some families where the women, within those narrow confines, appeared to have power and authority. However, our overwhelming conclusion is that there is no private domain for women nowadays. In so far as women are in the family, and the family is privatized, that domain does not afford woman any power: loneliness and isolation very often, but no domain to command or to share with other women. Klein proposes two kinds of families which she sums up diagrammatically. The first is traditional, with two spheres of activity, one for the man and one for the woman (1965 : 178). This is associated with another diagram in which the children are linked exclusively with the wife-mother. That latter diagram is contrasted with the second, emerging family form in which husband and wife are equally linked with the children. This is the emergence of the 'partnership' in the marriage.

Fathers in all social classes are now seen pushing prams much more than they were thirty years ago. Does this mean that there are now equal partnerships, that the 'democratic egalitarian family' has arrived? That women have equal power in the family with men? If they have this must in any case mean the loss for the women of any private domain that they might have had. And this is our conclusion: that the private domain has been invaded to the disadvantage of women but no equality of status in the public domain has yet been accorded them.

There are still those who have the domestic sphere to themselves: they lack freedom to enter the public domain but, living in a society without a female support group, simply find themselves imprisoned. Sally was one such. Sally, who lives in London and whose husband is a dustman, is oppressed and knows it. And she is understandably depressed. She has three children; her husbands expects her to wait on him. He comes home from work, eats, sleeps, baths, and goes to the pub where he stays until closing time. As Sally says, 'I'm domineered – my life's ruled for me' (Oakley 1974b : 155). Sally's husband not only does not help with the housework or the shopping or the baby except very occasionally, he also insists that she has the housework done before he comes in. Although he goes to the pub every day he does not let her out, except once a week to Bingo with *his* sister. Sally is never allowed to go dancing or to the pictures. She works because she needs the money, since he only gives her a set and limited amount each week, spending too much on drink.

Sally agrees with mothers working, but ' "I would never leave my children with someone they didn't know. You're going out to work *for* them; I mean if I didn't go out I couldn't afford to dress my children." ' Sally clearly has her own domain: she alone looks after everything to do with the house and the children. But this does not give her any power in the marital situation. On the contrary she says she regards her house as a prison. ' "My marriage is like boss and employee: I take my orders from my husband" ' (Oakley 1974b : 151). Sally is aware that other people have more companionship in their marriages. She is aware too that she is bringing her daughter up ready to accept a similar role and she regrets that she is doing this. Yet despite her unhappiness and her discontent, Sally is not prepared for any great changes. She does not at all agree that a husband should do the housework while a wife goes out to work. She would see such a man as a henpecked husband: ' "They should help *but not take over*" ' (Oakley 1974b : 155, our emphasis).

Much more common according to Oakley's work (1974a and 1974b) are various forms of 'sharing'. Oakley was essentially studying housework as an occupation which, as she says, has hitherto been little studied, perhaps because it is unpaid. Her studies reveal a great deal about the situation of women. Much of interest emerges about the relative power and powerlessness of housewives. Sally had a private domain in the sense that she alone did the housework and cared for the children, but she was powerless under the domination of her husband. Generally, Oakley's housewives expressed tensions about the extent to which they had any territory to command and the help their husbands might give them. Patricia, for example, resented the intrusions

123

on her territory ' "I don't polish properly on a Saturday and a Sunday because he's home and he don't like it." ' She doesn't mind the housework but she doesn't like being interrupted. But it isn't only the interruptions: ' "He'll come up in his hobnail boots when I'm washing the floor" ' (Oakley 1974b : 109). Patricia shares a quite commonly-held view that men are incompetent at housework, not suggesting, as Oakley (1974a) points out, that this might be from lack of practice.

What Patricia liked best about being a housewife was that 'you're your own boss', but she disliked most being taken for granted. She would not like a marriage where the man stayed home and did the housework. Such a husband would be a 'lazy sod' although earlier she had said that she thought women worked as hard as men. Although not so oppressed as Sally she still had an underlying feeling of being trapped: ' "if a man wants to go out for a drink he can just get up and go, we can't, can we . . . they'd have a lot to say about that, wouldn't they?" ' (Oakley 1974b : 113).

Margaret, who has a marriage that Oakley describes as 'egalitarian in ideology . . . effectively patriarchal in practice' also suffers from having little help and at the same time having her domain invaded. Her husband, she says, is very willing to help with the children but when it comes down to it, while he's willing to baby-sit, he's ' "very unreliable about getting home to do it" ' and while he will change a wet nappy, he won't change a dirty one. It's the same with housework. ' "He doesn't help now, but he did when I was working. Now I would have to ask him to wash up and he probably wouldn't do it. If we've had people to dinner he'll help me wash up then, and he'll also help me dish up which I find a bit embarrassing" ' (Oakley 1974b : 137). Margaret's husband thus invades her domain, takes from her the presentation of the food she has prepared for guests, and yet leaves her to undertake all the housewifely and mothering chores and works such long hours he is hardly ever home, although they do go out together at the weekends. Margaret does not have housekeeping money, ' "Peter just brings money home and puts it on the bedroom mantlepiece and we both take it. I haven't got a bank account. I don't want one" '. On occasions when she's used the Barclaycard she has felt she has had to ring her husband and confess. At the same time she says that not having money of her own ' "doesn't bother me really, because I'm never made to feel that Peter's the breadwinner and I'm totally dependent on him." ' Objectively, however, she obviously is. Overall she claims to be happy with her lot and likes being a mother. She thinks her husband works harder than she does. ' "I feel the man should be – not the domineering partner – but the *dominant* partner. I don't think women are inferior, but I think they're different . . . I'm glad I can look up to my husband" ' (Oakley 1974b : 140, emphasis in original.)

Juliet, a middle-class housewife, has similar problems but they are expressed rather differently. Before the baby came Juliet had shared her husband's domain: they worked together on films. Now she is excluded from his domain, left at home alone with the baby a great deal, and yet does not have command in the domestic sphere. She does not say so, but it is clear that he does not respect her skills in that sphere as being different from or greater than his own and she accepts his implicit judgement. This is quite unlike Patricia who is clear about male incompetence on all matters domestic. And it is quite unlike the more segregated families of the earlier British and Irish studies. As Goode (a man writing before the new phase of feminism, be it noted) pointed out, by sharing in the household chores the husband gains power, 'the household becoming a further domain for the exercise of prerogatives for making decisions' (Goode 1963 : 70).

Children

When speaking of women's power in the family it is clearly necessary to distinguish between power over husbands and power over children and to see to what extent women exercise power over children independently of men.

In rural Ireland and in Irish Liverpool, mothers had important amounts of influence, power, and authority over their children including their sons; influence and, in the Irish case sometimes power, which lasted into adulthood. In all societies where women are the child-rearers, all men are at one time subjected to the domination of their mothers. In the male-dominated mining town of Ashton this was broken when the men took over the boys

125

when they first went down the mine. All studies suggest that daughters stay closer to their mothers than do sons: the meaning and usefulness to the daughters and mothers of this closeness may vary, but it is clear that this is the gender order maintained. In contemporary urban society it is clear from evidence already adduced that men have invaded the female domain, including child-rearing. It is important to look at this situation more carefully however.

From Oakley's (1974b) respondents one learns that women do have some power over their children (and see Oakley 1974a : 14–16). Many feel that they do not want to leave their children to anyone else to bring up. As Patricia said ' "I wouldn't work at the moment: I wouldn't put Stephen anywhere, I'd wait until he was at school. Two years to go! I wouldn't want anyone else bringing them up, because I've seen too many children put out. I just don't believe in it" ' (Oakley 1974b : 107). The associated ideology of service is present at the same time: ' "If I worked it wouldn't be for myself, it'd be for *all* of us" ' (Oakley 1974b : 110, emphasis in the original). Her aim would be to save to buy a house. Not all women have this feeling of an exclusive right over their children. Juliet said that her husband would do anything you have to for a baby: he was very keen to learn. 'It's very much "our" baby' (Oakley 1974b : 121). At the same time she knew that a lot of husband-fathers did not behave in this way and the possible deviation of her husband from the norm worried her.

Because her husband is co-operative and helpful (helpful when he is there, that is, because his work takes him away from home for weeks at a time), child-rearing is not her exclusive domain. His help is also an invasion, bringing criticism with it.

' "The only trouble is that with the baby, the involvement goes to the extent that it's like a dual mother. He's the mother as well as me. He might come home for a week after being away filming, and he's giving her a drink while I'm cooking the meal, and he says, "Haven't you bought her any new teats – she hasn't had any for weeks!" That makes me angry because maybe I have bought some. There is criticism on that level. He gets very angry with me sometimes if I'm disorganized. Such silly things, as maybe I've bathed her but I haven't got her feed bottle hotted up which is stupid, because I've got a crying baby on my hands, or the bottle's too hot, and I haven't got any cold water to cool it down. It makes me angry too: it's terrible, all this unnecessary feeling." ' (1974b : 121–22)

Juliet would like to go back to work and would not mind sharing the upbringing of the baby, but then it is not her exclusive domain anyway. Even so, Juliet has no idea of taking a full-time career, and politics, although she does not mention it, would certainly not fit into the pattern she has in mind. For her ' " the main thing's worked out – getting married and having a baby" '.

Although Margaret was not keen to become a mother, now she has three children she is quite possessive about them. ' "Right up to the time I had [Lucy] I wasn't sure whether I would want her. I was even planning to put her in a nursery and go back to work. But the minute I saw her I loved her and I knew I couldn't let any one else look after her" ' (Oakley 1974a : 135).

The notion of children as property is not exclusive to the women. Oakley quotes the case of a father who was minding his eight-month-old baby for the afternoon and took him out: ' "He took him down to the Broadway, just carrying him – without a pushchair or anything – and he sat down for a rest on the way. He heard two women say "That's unusual, you don't often see a man out with a baby like that," and he said "It's my baby. Why *shouldn't* I take him out?" ' (Oakley 1974a : 158, emphasis in original).

These notions about women's responsibility for bringing up children have to been seen in the light of the increasing state interest in the proper rearing of children and the strong ideology associated with the work of John Bowlby about the 'need' that children have to be reared by their natural mothers. The present remarkable (and often unscientific) concern about 'bonding' reinforces his ideology. In a highly individualistic society children are resources which are valuable to their parents and which are also valuable to the state and to capitalist industry as future citizens and workers. It is no accident that state concern for the health and welfare of children began to develop when British industry was beginning to be overtaken in world markets for the first time and recruitment for the Boer War had revealed the unfitness of the male population.

In his perceptive paper on family and societal form, Harris argues that

> 'under conditions of a high degree of individuation charac-
> teristic of capitalism, the parents seek to reproduce not their
> society or their "house/line/family" but *themselves through*
> their children . . . the family . . . becomes not merely an
> agency of consumption, and of the reproduction of labour
> power, but a means of private production, a means of the
> reproduction of individuals into which society decomposes.'
> (Harris 1977 : 86–7, emphasis in original)

This arrangement, he argues, is shot through with contradictions, firstly that between the private and the communal nature
of children as products which leads to state interference in the
private affairs of the family, including taking over education. In
the second place 'the value of children, like that of all other
privately produced commodities, can only be realized when they
are exchanged. Parents are therefore confronted with a contradiction between their desire to possess their children and a desire
to realise their value' (Harris 1977 : 87).

If this argument is correct, and given the particular tasks performed by women in the division of labour in the nuclear family,
it can be argued that women have a material interest in rearing
their children themselves rather than delegating this task, for in
this way they can keep possession and control of their property, in
the case of many working-class families perhaps the only property they or their spouses have. The father also shares in this
property, but his control is less, since for much of the time he is
not there. When women delegate this task, they also lose day-to-
day control. This involves two risks: one, that a stranger, being
less concerned, may let an accident befall the child; the second is
similar, that the influence of a stranger may damage the child
morally and thus make it a less desirable and therefore less valuable member of the society and therefore less valuable property.

This argument suggests that what formerly was seen as the 'loss
of function of the family' (when for example, education was
taken over by the state) should better be seen as the removal from
the private female domain into the public male domain of an
activity in which women formerly had considerable power and

128

authority. Childbirth is another activity that has been expropriated from the private domain of the women. Births have been removed from the home, where they were predominantly under the control of women, to the hospital, where they are predominantly under the control of men. These changes have taken place at the behest of obstetricians (mostly men) and in the interests of reducing maternal and neo-natal mortality. At home a woman giving birth was 'queen for a day': everything in the household revolved around her labour. In hospital she is just another patient.

The teaching and ideology about the importance of early influences, associated with the already-existing lack of control from the school years onward, goes a good way to explain why so many women are prepared to compromise about going out to work when the children go to school. Even so, they wish to keep as much control as possible throughout that period and so are reluctant to take responsible work or work with long hours which would remove them as much as the father is already removed from the scene of child-rearing action. It should be noted that the children of the aristocracy and the bourgeoisie were already removed at a tender age from the influence of their mothers and put to schools which could be relied upon to train them to be appropriate male rulers. For this purpose, women, let alone women in the house, were not deemed appropriate. It would not be true to say that social class or education clearly co-varies with attitudes to child-rearing. Most studies show that working-class and middle-class mothers equally accept their maternal duties. Yet some middle-class mothers, being more highly educated, can command higher incomes and afford reasonably reliable child-minders. For a few, their loss of control over their children is compensated for by the increased material wealth and their increased influence in the public domain which, as several studies have suggested, increases women's power and influence in the family (Folsom 1948; Blood and Wolfe 1960; Gillespie 1972; Safilios-Rothschild 1969).

For Smith the problem of the oppression of children is a middle-class problem which derives from the sub-contractual relationship of the middle-class family to corporate capitalism, because the family is of crucial importance in socializing its children to the corporate mode: 'the children themselves become a product of the woman's activity in the home, and a mode therefore in which her activity is objectified' (Smith 1974 : 28) Good behaviour and good school performance are important and it is hard for parents to love the child who fails or behaves badly A woman has at one and the same time to bring her children up well and maintain a good family image however they behave The oppression of women, the oppression of children, and the oppression of children by women 'is a product of the woman's mediation to the child of the externalized order which in fact "oppresses" them both'. In this way 'the mother's service to her children becomes corrupted to a subordination of her children to that order. A mother's *failure* to mediate the external order to her children becomes proof that she does not love them' (Smith 1972 : 10, emphasis in original). Smith therefore disagrees with Firestone (1971) who argues that the common oppression of women and children is the basis of their ties.

Changing family law

In the last twenty years there have been considerable changes in family law all of which have generally been assumed to be part of the movement towards greater equality of the sexes and in favour of the 'democratic, egalitarian family'. What do the reforms do for the power of women in the home? There is no doubt that the new laws can be seen as following in the tendency of increased individualism.

The reforms have occurred in four areas: to protect the wife from violence or eviction by her husband; to replace 'matrimonial fault' by the notion of the 'irretrievable breakdown of marriage'; to improve, although not to equalize, the financial provision for wives on divorce; to improve the position of a wife or a woman when matrimonial property is being divided on death. The changes do not transform or abolish the family but offer 'a consolation to women for being in the family while strengthening the wife's position in the home, they do little to help get her out of the home' (Sachs and Wilson 1978 : 144). The social security legislation and regulations continue to be biased against women (Land 1976; Wilson 1977; Sachs and Wilson 1978).

The family law reflects what is understood to be the increasing tendency for marriages to be 'partnerships'; it in no way fundamentally alters the position of women as second-class citizens whose destiny is to serve their husbands and children in their families.

At the same time the rights of children over against their parents, including their mothers, have been increased, extending the notions of individuality to them. The relevant legislation has not reduced the dependency of children upon their parents: it has increased the circumstances in which agents of the state may act on behalf of children against the wishes of the parents. These increased state powers have been associated with a great deal of attention being paid to 'baby battering' although, as a cause of childhood injury and death, this is far outweighed by accidents, especially road accidents.

The question of feelings

Our arguments so far have ignored the issue of affect. Mothers report that they enjoy being with their children, although most report that sometimes the children get to be 'too much' and they are grateful for their husbands' occasional help. It is also reported that fathers enjoy their children and regret the work commitments that prevent them from seeing their children more often. The question of the emotions engendered within the family is an important one, both positive and negative emotions, and is a theme to which we will return in the final chapter. The feelings of women and men are clearly important, especially since as Oakley points out traditional notions of womanhood are central to the psychology of women (1974b : 195). She found (Oakley 1974b) that, in 1971 when her interviews were carried out, the majority of women reacted unfavourably to the notions of women's liberation. They clung quite closely to the domestic female role and the associated female virtues. Sally, the dustman's wife, perhaps stated the case more dramatically than some of the others, but she makes it very plain. She said that although women were not inferior they would 'never be as equal' as men. She did not fancy thinking of herself as humping sacks of rubbish about. 'If it's equality so far as women MPs, why not women

131

dustmen? And I don't think women could do it. So I therefore say men are the stronger sex in some things, but not in all things.' Quite apart, therefore, from the circumstances of her prison home which would make it impossible for her to take up any sort of political career, Sally does not approve of women MPs. Politics is not for women, 'They couldn't do it' (Oakley 1974b : 155).

We conclude that women have some, but not much power in the family and that that power has diminished. Most power is in the hands of men and we agree with Hunt (1978b : 557) that it is a question of power rather than authority. We conclude also that the privatized nuclear family embedded in capitalist society maintains children's and women's lack of freedom. Individualism, the ideology at the heart of capitalism, stresses the reproduction of individuals in this group, as Harris has argued. Women are locked into these isolated units, gaining their only power and influence there over the children of both sexes who are initially even more dependent than their mothers are, but who will later leave them bereft and role-less. True it may be that women can then enter the public world, but at what a disadvantage in terms of training and experience compared with their male peers who have been there continuously for many years.

SEVEN

Women in public power: fifty years on

'The near-universal recognition of women's political rights and the strength of their voting numbers in many countries are nowhere reflected in their direct role in government. An enormous disparity exists between women's formal political equality and their meaningful exercise of political power. Though 99.5 per cent of the women in the world are legally entitled to participate in the political process, the numbers of women in public office remain in most countries appallingly low.' (Newland 1975 : 8, 9)

' "I think women tend to see things differently to men – a different point of view and sometimes a more practical point of view than a man. But men like to think they're better. I don't know why – I suppose that's life really, isn't it?" ' (Chamberlain 1977 : 135–36)

If women have lost power in the private domain as a result of the developments of individualism, capitalism, and an ever more intrusive state, how have they fared in the public domain? The answer in terms of power, prestige, and influence is that they have not fared at all well, although women's involvement in the public domain has undoubtedly increased.

Women now constitute over 40 per cent of the labour force: in 1978 there were almost 9,200,000 employed women (TUC 1979 : 11). While it seems clear, as Beechey (1977) has argued, that women's waged labour has been used as a 'reserve army' to cushion production problems in wars or in response to other economic demands, it has to be made plain that women, including married women, now play a critical part in the labour force. To this extent women are no longer privatized at home. They have entered in considerable numbers into the world of work which was formerly, in some parts of the country at least, as in the Banbury of 1950, 'a man's world' (Stacey 1960). There is an apparent great change in the employment of *married* women who by 1974 comprised nearly a quarter of the working population compared with 13 per cent in 1951. It is estimated that by 1986 nearly two-thirds of married women aged between thirty-five and fifty-nine years of age will be working compared with one in five in 1951 (Land 1976). (Although this prediction may not be fulfilled given the present recession and renewed 'back-to-the-home' pressure upon married women.)

Housewives still

The change in one sense is more apparent than real. A comparison of the work pattern of women in Banbury between 1951 and 1966 showed that while few married women worked in 1951, it had become the norm by 1966. But this did not mean that women had uninterrupted working lives. The most common pattern was for women to work until their first child was born and then return to work either when their last child entered school or left school. Their primary task as child-bearers and child-rearers was retained and for them now there were two tasks to be done, running the home and earning a living. It is in the context of these changes that sociological work about women in the period

134

immediately after the Second World War and for twenty-five years thereafter concentrated on 'women's two roles' (Williams (1945), Myrdal and Klein (1956), the Rapoports (1971), Young and Wilmott (1973) – the latter painting a quite unrealistically optimistic picture of the nuclear family becoming symmetrical while all the evidence suggests it remains stubbornly asymmetrical. See Chapter 6, above, and Gillespie (1972)). Hunt (1978a, 1980) has made a new departure recently studying in some detail the relationship between domestic work and paid work and how these were integrated among couples in North Staffordshire. Although not all her couples conform to the dominant ideologies she found that these still were that the man is the breadwinner and the woman the home-maker.

Working mothers' problems

The strains between the two roles continue, and discussion has now moved from the textbooks to the popular press. A survey done for *Women's Own* early in 1979 by Social Surveys (Gallup Poll) Ltd found 966 mothers in a representative sample of 4,000. Six hundred and one of the 966 mothers went out to work or wanted to. The final results, which were based on interviews with 512 mothers, showed that of the mothers of children aged between five and sixteen, 15 per cent worked full time, 37 per cent did not work but would have liked to, 7 per cent were not sure, and 21 per cent did not work and did not want to. Of those mothers with children under five years, 6 per cent worked full time, 18 per cent worked part-time, 27 per cent did not work but would have liked to, 8 per cent were not sure, 41 per cent did not work and did not want to (*Woman's Own* 1979 : 22).

The *Woman's Own* decision to run a campaign on behalf of working mothers suggests that major structural changes have taken place in the society which are causing difficulties and discontents for a large number of ordinary women, for *Woman's Own* can hardly be described as a 'women's lib.' publication. A similar discontent with the trappings without the substance of equality, and also echoing the reality of women's work, was revealed by the large response to the campaign to equalize tax conditions for married women with those of men, whether married or single, and single women, run by the *Sunday Times* in 1978.

Women have entered the public world but have not been accorded equality with men in that world. Married women continue to be those most discriminated against, further evidence in support of our thesis that it is the institution of the family in its present form that has prevented women's full entry as individuals into the public arena.

'Women's work'

As several writers have made plain, when women go out to work they tend to find it in particular kinds of jobs: textiles; hotel and catering; shop work and light engineering; clerical work; in short, women do women's work (Oakley 1974b; Mackie and Pattullo 1977). It continues to be paid less than men's work on average, despite the Equal Pay and Sex Discrimination Acts and most women are subservient to men in their work.

Women in management

Furthermore, women much more rarely achieve managerial positions; when they do, they are much more likely to be in middle and junior management than genuine policy-making positions (Fogarty, Rapoport, and Rapoport 1971a, 1971b). To give just two examples: one large engineering firm employing 15,000 women in a total workforce of 50,000 in 1975 had thirty-five women in managerial grades out of 4,784 people. In one of the largest national insurance companies, where women comprised over 30 per cent of employees, less than 1 per cent of women employees were in managerial posts compared to 17 per cent of the men (Mackie and Pattullo 1977 : 76).

This situation is not confined to Britain. While the number of women in employment in the United States rose from 14 million in 1940 to over 40 million in 1977, men 'managers and administrators' outnumbered the women by five to one; only 3 per cent of all working women were in such posts (Finkelstein 1980 : 193). Women form a tiny minority of those at the very highest levels in the largest corporations. In some 1,300 of the largest (industrial and non-industrial) corporations in the United States in 1972 'there were 6,500 officers and directors earning over $30,000 of whom *eleven* . . . were women!' (Korda 1978 : 185, emphasis in original).

Helge Pross has argued that while top management in large corporations in West Germany is almost exclusively a male affair, women do better as independent entrepreneurs. That is, they are better represented among small business owners who are not part of the national economic elite (Pross 1980 : 212). Carol Finkelstein (1980) argues for the importance of family business connections in the backgrounds of enterprising women in most historical periods. She is able to trace a pattern in the USA up to the mid-seventies in which women have been spurred to enterprise by a family crisis such as the death or absence of a male relative. Seven of the 'Ten most important women in big business' chosen by *Fortune Magazine* in 1973 were in family businesses (p. 195).

In such enterprises there is not the clear distinction between the private and public domains that there is in the large-scale corporation. The greater success of women in business in such families is consistent with our hypothesis that the separation of the public and private domains is particularly disadvantageous for women.

The decline of the family business and the rise of professional management are therefore of considerable significance for women's entry to business elites. The influence that women could exert in a family business is not possible in a depersonalized bureaucratic corporation. Women have not been compensated for this loss: accorded citizenship but still defined by their position in the family, they have had difficulty in competing as equals with men for entry to and promotion in this modern world of business administration. On the contrary, as we saw in the last chapter, they are used by business corporations to support (unpaid) their husbands who are the managers and to rear their children in an appropriate manner. It must be remembered that the transfer of ownership of assets to women (as family members) simply for accounting purposes does not give women more than 'paper ownership'. The crucial test is whether women figure prominently at board level, especially in executive positions.

137

Women in the professions

Nor, sixty years after the removal of disqualifications to entry, are women prominent in senior positions in the professions. They have long had a place there in those areas concerned with 'women's affairs' which are most closely associated with their assumed 'natural' role of caring for and serving others. But even where women are in a substantial proportion or even a majority of posts, senior and management posts go disproportionately to men. Such is the case in social work, nursing, and teaching. Thus, a third of top nursing posts are held by men, who make up around 10 per cent of nurses (Mackie and Pattullo 1977 : 73). Moves towards professionalism and new career structures attract more competition from the men (Carpenter 1977). In the 'caring profession' of social work, 60 per cent of field staff are women, 60 per cent of management posts are held by men. By April 1971, following reorganization in local authority social services departments, out of 160 appointments to posts of Director of Social Services, there were fourteen women. In 1975, out of 116 Directors, eleven were women (Clarke 1978 : 22). By a similar logic, the advent of scientific management has increased the competition from men in the field of personnel management. In 1970, the Institute of Personnel Management had a female membership of 19 per cent compared with 25 per cent in 1965. Commenting on this decline, the Institute felt that personnel management was now part of 'the managerial aspect which society accepted as a male function' (Mackie and Pattullo 1977 : 78), a process of 'defeminization'.

While considerable progress has been made in opening up the prestigious and traditionally male-dominated professions to women, the battle is very far from being won. Women comprise under 1 per cent of bank managers, 2 per cent of chartered accountants and university professors, and 5 per cent of architects (Oakley 1979a : 392). The realm of law, as Sachs and Wilson have shown, is overwhelmingly male. While law offices depend on low-paid clerical workers (mostly women), the great majority of senior lawyers are men. In 1976, women comprised 8.8 per cent of barristers and 4.5 per cent of practising solicitors. Five out of 265 circuit judges were women and two out of seventy

High Court Judges. There was no woman among the Law Lords and Court of Appeal (Sachs and Wilson 1978 : 174, 175).

Women and trade unions: increased membership unrepresented in leadership

If women have not risen to many positions of power or influence in industry or the professions, how have they fared in the trade union movement? The changes in the nature and extent of women's paid work have been reflected in the trade unions. Women's employment and membership have been stimulated by war; women's membership trebled during the First World War and doubled in the Second World War (Mackie and Pattullo 1977 : 165). While there is a tendency for their employment opportunities and membership to slip back in peace-time, the continued need for women workers after the Second War has meant that they have been a major source of recruitment for the unions in recent years. Between 1960 and 1978, female membership of the TUC rose by more than two million and accounted for 55 per cent of the total increase. (It is important to remember in this regard that unions with relatively large female memberships such as NALGO and NUT affiliated in this period.) In 1960 women comprised 16.5 per cent of the total affiliated membership compared to 28.7 per cent in 1978 when the number of women members stood at 3,411,000 (TUC 1979; Appendix A). In the last fifty years, the proportion of female members in the TUC has almost trebled (see Appendix: *Table 3*). This increase not only reflects the increase in the number of women in employment but also an increase in the proportion of the female workforce which is in the trade union movement though it is still substantially less than for male workers. In 1958 approximately 24 per cent of women workers were in trade unions compared with 34 per cent in 1973. In the latter year, the comparable figure for male workers was 60 per cent, or an increase of just under 6 per cent on the 1953 figure (McCarthy 1977 : 163).

The largest growth in women's membership has occurred in the public sector, which is easier to organize than the private sector and where there is less difficulty in securing employer recognition (McCarthy 1977 : 165, 166). Women also tend to be increasingly concentrated in comparatively few unions, a fact which reflects their concentration in a narrow range of jobs in a limited number of industries. In 1978, the 'top ten' unions, that is, those with the highest numbers of women members, together accounted for 72 per cent of the total number of women in TUC unions. NUPE, for example, had more than 450,000 women members and NALGO, NUGMW, and TGWU well over 300,000 each (TUC 1979 : Appendix A).

The overall growth in women's membership and the substantial proportion of women in some of the larger unions have not been reproduced at leadership levels. In 1975, when one trade union member in every three was a woman, the ratio of male to female full-time officers was thirty-two to one. In the TGWU in 1976, when women comprised approximately one-fifth of total membership, there were three full-time women officials out of some 480, no women executive members, and two women TUC delegates out of seventy-eight. In the GMWU, almost half of the members were women, yet only ten of the 282 full-time officials were women and none of the executive members; of 68 delegates to the TUC only four were women (*Spare Rib* 1977). In unions where women members outnumber men, the situation is no better. In 1978 COHSE, with two-thirds female membership, had one paid woman official and NUPE, with 62 per cent women, had none (*Observer* 1976).

Women in the movement are conscious of their lack of representation at Congress. While one in every 11,900 trade unionists could be a delegate to the 1978 Congress, the ratio for men was 1 : 7,800 compared with 1 : 38,800 for women. In that Congress, there were eighty-eight women among the 1,172 delegates (7.5 per cent) whereas there had been forty-seven out of 1,051 (4.5 per cent) in 1968. Despite this small advance, only thirty of the 115 unions represented there included a woman delegate (TUC 1979 : 32, 33).

Women in administration

Despite some gains in the Civil Service, especially during the Second World War, whereby women entered most areas on formally equal terms with men, the higher levels of responsibility

140

and reward have continued to elude women (Kelsall 1955 : 4–9). Women have sought entry to administrative grades in increasing numbers in recent years but they have made little progress. Sixty years after the Sex Disqualification (Removal) Act, they remain concentrated in the lowest grades: 79 per cent of the bottom grade, Clerical Assistant, are women; 35 per cent of Executive Officers; 7.7 per cent of Senior Executive Officers; 4.1 per cent of Under Secretaries; and 2.7 per cent of Deputy Secretaries are women. There is no woman Permanent Under Secretary (*Guardian* 1979).

Women and politics in Britain

The number of women representatives at the national level has not increased dramatically over the last fifty years. Women have yet to reach the level of 5 per cent of candidates returned to Westminster in any one general election.

Between the wars, the number of women MPs increased slowly from one in 1919 to a peak of fifteen in 1931 before falling to nine in 1935. After the war, the twenty-four successes in the 1945 General Election seemed to augur well for women. In fact the number of women reached a plateau in the years 1955 to 1974 when their number did not rise above twenty-nine nor fall below twenty-three. In 1979, the year of election of the first woman Prime Minister, the number of women slumped to nineteen; not since 1951 have there been so few women in the House.

Women have also been slow to gain election in local government. In the last year for which official data is available, women comprised 12 per cent of successful candidates in local government (Royal Commission on Local Government in England 1969). While parity with men is still a long way off, this represents a greater degree of success than their counterparts in central government where the comparative figure for women in Parliament in the same period was 4.6 per cent.

Experience in local government has been important in the backgrounds of many eminent political women who have gone on to higher things, as both Currell (1974) and McCowan (1975) show. While it represents a highly important first stage in the recruitment and training of many women MPs, some prefer to

141

head straight for Westminster (Vallance 1979). However if women's participation rises noticeably, although still far from parity with men, there is talk of the 'feminization' of the assembly or body in question. Sullerot suggests that such fears were expressed about the Greater London Council when women made up 20 per cent of members in 1975 (Sullerot 1977 : 42).

The relative success of women in the direct elections to the European Assembly suggests that this is not seen as a prestigious or influential body. This is confirmed by the overall turnout on the part of the British electorate, which was nearer that for a local than a general election. Of the 265 candidates in Great Britain, twenty-four were women, that is just over 9 per cent, and women gained ten of the seventy-eight seats (13 per cent). They did considerably better than their contemporaries in the national general election in the same summer (1979) where women were just 3 per cent of successful candidates. The overall total of women in the Assembly was sixty-seven out of 410 (16 per cent).

The same the whole world over

Throughout the world, as Kathleen Newland has remarked in the quotation at the head of this chapter, there is an 'enormous disparity between women's formal political equality and their meaningful exercise of political power' (1975 : 8, 9). In common with other such reviews (Duverger 1955; Milburn 1976; Iglitzin and Ross 1976; Sullerot 1977), she presents a depressingly familiar picture of women's lack of progress in political and civil life throughout the world. This statement is in no way vitiated by the presence of women prime ministers in Britain and India. Indeed it is only because of the almost complete absence of women in high political office that Mrs Thatcher, Mrs Ghandi, and, in her day, Mrs Golda Meir, are so highly visible.

Newland's survey of the proportion of seats held by women in thirty-five national legislative bodies reveals that women rarely account for as much as 10 per cent of total membership (Newland 1975 : 9). In 1975 the proportion of women in national legislatures in Latin America ranged from none in Panama to 8 per cent in Mexico. In Africa and the Middle East in 1973, the proportion ranged from none in Lebanon to 7 per cent in Israel and 27 per cent in Guinea (1975). In Asia, fifteen of the 313 seats of the Bangladesh Parliament were reserved for women while women made up 5 per cent of the Indian Parliament (1975) and 2 per cent of the Japanese House of Representatives (1970). In Western Europe and North America in 1975, women accounted for 7 per cent of members in the West German Bundestag, 3 per cent of the United States Congress and 2 per cent of the Greek Chamber of Deputies (Appendix B).

The main exceptions to the 'ten per cent rule' were in Scandinavia, where the proportion of women in 1975 was 22 per cent in Finland, 21 per cent in Sweden, and 17 per cent in Denmark, and in certain one-party systems, including the Soviet Union, the Eastern European countries, and developing countries like China and Guinea.

Newland (1975) points out that in most of the one-party states membership of the legislature is less important as a centre of real power than position in the party (p. 9). In 1975 35 per cent of members in the Russian Supreme Soviet were women but there were only 2 per cent women in the party Central Committee (241 members), and no women among the ninety-two members of the Council of Ministers and the twenty-two members of the Politburo (p. 39).

The under-representation of women in the party hierarchies in such countries severely limits the women's chances of a political career and their opportunities for influencing government. This is not to deny that in both Russia and China women have made substantial progress since their respective revolutions. As Rowbotham (1972) has argued, it is difficult for us to imagine the extent of their subordination and degradation under the old order. In comparison, the advances in social, political, economic, and civil freedoms for women are enormous; indeed the recognition that they were persons was in itself revolutionary. Today, however, male control of the party hierarchy, and through this, of all aspects of public life, severely reduces any hope of equality of status for women in public affairs. In the Soviet Union, the proportion of women among party members is less than one in four and, as Newland argues, even this is possibly substantially better than the equivalent figure for China (p. 17).

In those countries where the activities of political parties are more concerned with electoral politics, Newland concludes that women are usually absent from policy-making and leadership positions: 'Most women who participate in party activities are cannon-fodder; they knock on doors, answer telephones, hand out leaflets, and get out the vote – usually in the service of a male candidate' (pp. 22, 23).

This judgement compares closely with that of the Labour Party Study Group:

> 'Whilst there is no discernable prejudice against women as voluntary workers at grass roots level in political parties (where their fund raising and educational work is much needed and accepted), there are remarkably few women to be found either in Parliament or in the top levels of the party organization.' (The Labour Party 1972 : 34)

In all areas of public life, in elected and appointed offices, at local as well as national level, in parties and pressure groups, women have a secondary, if not a subservient, position. The proportion of women decreases as we move from the lowest ranks of political and public organizations to the higher levels. Such is the case, as Newland demonstrates, in Civil Service hierarchies (Newland 1975 : 12, 13) and in systems of appointment to public office (1975 : 11). And there is more room for women in local than in national government (1975 : 15).

The under-representation of women is particularly marked in international organizations whatever their size, purpose, powers, or structures (unless like the European Assembly they are discredited or they are organized by women for women). The United Nations is not exceptional in spite of all its official pronouncements on the status of women. In 1974, as Betsy Thom (1980) reports, women comprised 8.3 per cent of delegates to the UN General Assembly (1980 : 175) and 10.3 per cent of staff members in Permanent Missions (1980 : 174). The last figure is especially significant since Permanent Missions play a central role in shaping UN personnel policies, including the composition of the Secretariat (1980 : 175).

But some are more political than others

In an earlier chapter we argued that where there was strict segregation into a woman's domain and a man's public domain women exercised quite extensive influence and some power through their structural position in their domain and through the informal networks of women. In such countries women have made least progress in entering the public political domain; not surprisingly, since the notion of women as independent persons is no part of the structure or culture.

Elsa Chaney (1973) has examined this lack of progress in public affairs and the tentative nature of women's commitment to public affairs. Chaney shows that women in the late sixties in both 'progressive' Chile and 'traditional' Peru, in common with women throughout Latin America, were severely under-represented in the public domain, which both men and women agreed was no place for women. They were the least economi-cally active of women in any major world region (1973 : 106). Even when young and single, few women worked outside the home. They could only achieve honour as wives and mothers.

Only a tiny minority of women hold office. Chaney estimated that women occupied 1.5 per cent of all Cabinet posts in Latin countries. Moreover women have been slow to use their right to vote. In Chile they did not begin to vote in significant numbers even in local elections until fifteen years after enfranchisement. In the mid 1960s, only 61 per cent of women of voting age were registered: this, however was still almost twice that for Peruvian women (1973 : 110). In both countries, women tended to defer to their husbands' judgement in political matters (1973 : 112).

This contrasts with Newland's report that in a 1975 sample, 73 per cent of voters in the United States, compared with less than a third in 1931, said they would vote for a qualified woman candi-date for President (Newland 1975 : 30). This as Newland con-cludes, despite the remaining hurdles, indicates that 'women's rights' is becoming a respectable issue.

Women in the parties in Britain

At national, local, and international level much depends on the position of women in the political parties and the party elites' attitudes, prejudices, and opinions on the role of women in politics. Nowhere has a 'woman's party' developed. It is in the parties that candidates are put forward for election and for appointment to other public bodies. All the parties include women in their membership. But there are few women to be found in the top levels of either the constituency or national party organizations.

The Labour Party Study Group reported in its Green Paper on discrimination against women (1972) that there were only seven women out of a total elected membership of twenty-six on the National Executive Committee of the Labour Party (of the seven occupied seats five are reserved for women) and that women delegates had made up only 10.6 per cent of all those at the 1971 National Conference (Labour Party 1972 : 34). There had been only ten women chairmen of the party out of a total of seventy (1972 : 35).

At first sight, the situation of women within the Conservative Party seems more encouraging. According to the same report, the National Union's much larger executive committee of almost 200 members included nearly fifty women in 1971 and there were nine women among the sixty members of the General Purposes Committee. There is also special provision for a woman delegate from each constituency to National Conference. But there were only four women out of a total membership of twenty-seven on the very important Advisory Committee on Policy which is responsible solely to the Conservative leader (Labour Party 1972 : 35). By 1975 there had been fifteen women chairmen (sic) and four women Presidents of the National Union (Sturges-Jones 1975 : 18, 19). In the middle of all the publicity surrounding Margaret Thatcher's entry to No. 10 in 1979, few people noticed that several other women had lost their seats or that there had otherwise been a modest increase of one in the Conservative women's ranks. Mrs Thatcher's advisers and cabinet colleagues are men. Reporting on her choice of cabinet, the press headlines read, 'All Maggie's Men' (*The Observer*, 6 May) and 'Maggie's Men for the Eighties' (*Daily Mail*, 7 May).

In spite of the rhetoric of the parties and their differences in structure and organization, both provide further evidence of women's absence from powerful positions. It is not therefore surprising that women are under-represented among candidates, themselves part of the party elite. It is a disappointing record (see Appendix: *Table 1*). In 1929 1.7 per cent of Conservative parliamentary candidates were women; in 1979, just 5 per cent. Figures for Labour candidates were 5.3 per cent in 1929 and only 8.2 per cent in 1979. Labour have consistently fielded a higher proportion of women candidates since 1918. The Liberal party has been more generous to women in terms of candidates than either of the two major parties in the post-war period.

It would be a mistake to conclude that the increase in the total number of women candidates, from sixty-nine in 1929 to 212 in 1979, indicates remarkable progress for women. In proportionate terms it represents an increase from 4 per cent of all candidates in 1929 to just over 8 per cent in 1979. The increase in the *number* of women candidates in recent years reflects a more general increase in the number of candidates fielded by minor parties. In 1979 for example Liberal and other minor parties fielded 1,330 candidates or 52 per cent of all candidates compared to 142 or 10 per cent of all candidates in 1951. This growth has been especially striking in the seventies. One result has been an increase in the number of women candidates. In the four general elections in that decade, these other parties offered the electorate 161 female candidates compared to twenty in the four preceding elections.

It is important to remember that these are parties in which candidates have very little real hope of electoral success. Women have the best chances of securing candidacies in parties which are unlikely to win elections: as the chances of reward increase, competition from the men increases. Following the success and expansion of the Scottish National Party in the early seventies, the number of women candidates declined. One party worker observed:

> ' "It really does seem as if the more successful we become the more fierce the male competition becomes. There was much more scope in the early days for women on the candidates' list because men had more of an eye on the main chance and didn't fancy being failed candidates. But the number of women candidates has conspicuously dropped since the SNP stopped being simply a quixotic venture. " ' (Mackie and Pattullo 1977 : 80).

The women tend to be left 'showing the flag' in the hopeless seats.

The greater the chance of success, the less likely, on average is the candidate to be a woman especially since women are less likely than men to be selected to fight safe or winnable seats (see p. 162). Currell, following Ross (1953) shows that for a very long time the average woman candidate was less than half as likely as the average man candidate to be successful in a general election. From 1951 up to and including the general election of 1970, she concludes that these differences in prospects have narrowed until there was almost no difference between the sexes in 1970 (Currell 1974 : 27). But this trend has been reversed in the seventies. In 1979, women candidates on average were once more much less likely to succeed than their male counterparts.

The finding that the closer to power, the fewer the women, also holds for the field of public appointments. The under-representation of women is characteristic of all those organizations and public bodies that have so much to do with the administration of the 'mixed economy' and the 'welfare state'.

Women have not shared in the remarkable growth of such bodies in the postwar period. To take just a few examples: the Manpower (sic) Services Commission, whose members are appointed by the Secretary of State for Employment following consultation with the CBI, the TUC, and Local Authority associations, had one woman out of ten members in 1978. Similarly, the Advisory, Conciliation and Arbitration Service had one woman councillor out of nine in 1979; the Science Research Council had not a single woman among its thirteen members, the Medical Research Council had just one woman out of seventeen, the Social Science Research Council two women out of seventeen, and the reformed General Medical Council, eight women out of a total membership of ninety-three. Of the 425 members of forty-one public boards of a commercial character in 1978, we find just twenty-eight women (6.6 per cent). The Post Office had two women out of a total membership of eighteen; British Airways had one woman out of fifteen members, and the National Enterprise Board, one out of eleven. Many boards had no women at all, including the Electricity Board, the British Gas Corporation, British Rail and the Scottish and Welsh Development Agencies (Civil Service Department 1978).

If present at all, women are more often found in less important and less influential bodies, at local or regional rather than national level, and on advisory rather than decision-making bodies. This, for example, is true of Social and National Health Service groups at local level. Women comprised approximately one quarter of members of RHAs in 1979 while a sample survey indicated that they made up 43 per cent of members of the local, less powerful Community Health Councils (Klein and Lewis 1976 : 178). But even there only 31 per cent of vice-chairpersons and 22 per cent of chairpersons were women: the higher the position, the less likely is the occupant to be a woman.

While we hesitate to include the House of Lords in this class of appointment, since the Life Peerages Act (1958) its methods of recruitment have not been unlike those of other public bodies. Women are under-represented among life peers. In 1979 there were thirty-nine women among a total of 303 life peers, or 13 per cent. While still very much a minority, it is, significantly, a better proportion than that in the more powerful Lower House (Whittaker's Almanac 1979). In the Upper House as a whole, women form an even smaller minority due to the persistence of the hereditary element: in 1978, there were seventeen peeresses in their own right, comprising less than 2 per cent of the Hereditary Peerage. There were no women among the Lords Spiritual or the Law Lords.

How come so many made it?

We argued earlier that it is surprising how much progress women have made in the public domain. Given all the evidence how can we say this? First of all it is clear from the data we have reviewed in this chapter so far that women are no longer entirely privatized, as women in the upper, middle, and artisan classes at one time were. Women have entered the work-force in large numbers. Furthermore there are only limited areas, like the highest ranks of the law and the priesthood of the Anglican and Roman Catholic Churches, where no women are to be found. Before we can justify our assertion that women have come a long way, we have to show that women are now acting as individuals in the public

149

domain, for it was that that we thought was radical – action as an individual and not as daughter, wife, or mother.

At the outset, however, it is important to realize what a small minority of people we are talking about when we are discussing power in the public domain. Only a minority of the population are involved in executive and managerial decisions, in making public policy. Even when one comes to the 'mass movements' on which democratic government is based, only a minority of the population is involved: politics is not a game many people choose to play. While there may be few women compared to men in the game, the number of male players is small in relation to the total population. We have shown that the senior management and administration in the public and private sectors are largely composed of men: a few of the men govern, through industry, commerce, services or the state, many facets of the lives of the great majority of women and men. A few women have come to be involved. How did they get there? What keeps the others out? Why do not more women come forward? Is it reluctance to serve or inability to enter the higher reaches of the public domain that accounts for this state of affairs that where the power is there the women are not? It is important to have an answer to these questions to guide women who wish to share more fully in the public domain as to the strategies they should adopt. It is particularly important to know the extent to which the women who succeed in the public arena are 'exceptional' (cf. Mitchell 1971 : 129). If we believe that any woman can make it if she tries, then the strategies that the women's movement and individual women might follow would be quite different from those that would follow the belief that given the present social order, specifically the gender order, women, other than a few exceptional women, just cannot win.

An attempt to answer these questions must be made at two levels. First there is the general social level of the major social institutions of the society and the ideologies that support them. Second is the level of the specific social processes, social relations, attitudes, and ideas involved in entering and achieving positions of power in the public domain. At the general level we have argued that until recently any power and influence which women might be able to exert they derived from their positions as

150

members of family or kin groups; that to enter the public domain as individuals in their own right is a radical step. In making this attempt women are faced with a pre-existing gender order and the ideologies which sustain it, an order in which men dominate in the public domain.

Division of labour in the family

In our view, as long as the attitudes to women's status and obligations and the division of labour in the family remain unchanged, it is difficult to believe that gender will be irrelevant to politics. We have argued elsewhere (Stacey and Price 1979) that legislation is not enough to establish a gender order in which women are seen as the equals of men. Legislation alone cannot overturn the ideologies and assumptions underpinning male domination, which are rarely spoken and which seem so natural to those who hold them that they are not aware of them. When these assumptions are challenged in some way, as they are when women attempt to enter positions of leadership in public affairs, people experience acute discomfort. Nor can legislation for equality alter the division of labour with regard to housework and child rearing. That requires positive social intervention of another kind: the provision of alternative child-care arrangements, for example. In practice, legislation in these fifty years has reinforced the pre-existing gender order. The Beveridge reforms were based on the assumption that women should be and wanted to be first and foremost, wives and mothers. Women in the family have been faced with an increasing number of professional experts, acting as agents of the state (but also offering barrages of advice from commercial sources) as to how they should serve their husbands, run their houses, and rear their children. Hilary Graham (1979) has shown how preventive health interventions can raise anxieties of mothers about their child-rearing practices.

As Elizabeth Wilson puts it, 'Social welfare policies amount to no less than the *State organization of domestic life*' (Wilson 1977 : 9, emphasis in original). Woman's responsibility to work in the home has been constantly reinforced at the same time as her faith in her domestic abilities and 'natural' skills has been undermined (cf. Ehrenreich and English 1979).

The incompatibility of the family and public life

The upshot is an inbuilt incompatibility between the notions of what it is to be a woman and what is required of people in public life. Women may only share simultaneously in the public and private domains in circumstances in which they either have few obligations in the private domain or few responsibilities in the public domain, so that their domestic responsibilities may always be able to take precedence. This notion was made plain by Colonel Applin in 1928, objecting

> 'to the – clearly abominable – possibility of a woman Chancellor of the Exchequer. To Miss Wilkinson's "Why not?" he riposted with relentless logic, "Imagine in the middle of her (Budget) speech a message coming in, ' – Your child is dangerously ill. Come at once – ' I should like to know how much of that Budget the House would get, and what the figures would be like." ' (Vallance 1979)

The early women pioneers who believed and hoped that women's contribution to public life would eliminate prejudice were mistaken. Fifty years later the evidence is that women's position in the family is rarely irrelevant to an assessment of their suitability for positions in the public domain. Women cannot meet obligations in one area without being accused of neglecting duties in the other; the qualities associated with the competent performance of roles in one sphere are deemed inappropriate for success in the other. As Epstein has it:

> 'Women who do manage to marshall their energies and support from their families often face hostile and condescending attitudes . . . because they must withdraw from family responsibilities, as men do, during a campaign.
>
> Although male candidates usually try to show that they have strong family ties and the support of wives and children, they seldom face questioning from the electorate as to the quality or extent of the care that they give their children or the

affection that they give their wives. A woman is caught in what has been described as a "double bind": if she campaigns vigorously, she is apt to be criticized as a neglectful wife and mother; if she claims to be an attentive mother, her ability to devote time and energy to public office is questioned' (Epstein 1980 : 126).

There are many other ways in which relationships between spouses and actual or assumed responsibilities for children take on different meanings for the sexes in the public domain. So deep-seated and pervasive are the assumptions about a 'woman's proper place', that differential treatment continues in spite of legislation and codes of conduct designed to reduce discrimination against women.

Women's proper place

Women themselves share in these deep-seated beliefs and feelings and, at least while their children are young, are anxious to be available, all those women, that is, who are not in a position to provide alternative care. Cultural conservatism is by no means confined to the men. Women as well as men continue to believe that political and public affairs are male domains. In the roles they adopt in the family, in their differential upbringing of their boy and girl children, women help to perpetuate a gender order that ensures a subservient place and a secondary position in public affairs for women. It is not easy to tell how far the cultural conservatism on the part of women is the result of the unavailability of alternative social arrangements and women's inability in the face of strongly dominant norms to be able to imagine alternatives, let alone invent them, given their relatively slender resources.

The educational system continues to play its part in maintaining the notions of women's proper place and women's work. While the number of women holding new awards at Universities rose by 211 per cent in the period 1960 to 1972 (compared with a male growth rate of 154 per cent), men still outnumber women by 2 : 1. Patterns of subject specialization are greatly influenced by traditional notions of sex roles (Oakley 1979 : 392). Girls still

153

study 'girls' subjects' (Byrne 1978; Deem 1978; Wolpe 1978). Women are less often expected or encouraged than are men to proceed from undergraduate to graduate work.

Even Mrs Thatcher supports the traditional woman's role. During her 1979 election campaign she said:

> 'I didn't get there by being some strident female. I don't like strident females. I like people who have ability, who don't run the feminist ticket too hard. After all, it's not because of your sex that you get anywhere, its because of your ability as a person.' (*Daily Mail*, 27 April 1979)

The clear implication is that there are no structural barriers to the advancement of women in public life and that progress can be achieved without alterations in the institution of the family and the division of labour there between the sexes. Women can remain 'feminine' and not 'strident', run a home, attend to their family, and develop the qualifications, commitment, and self-confidence to run for political office. The Conservative pamphleteer Sue McCowan supports the view that more women should enter public life but this must and can be achieved without detriment to 'family life':

> 'This is not a call for women to abandon their homes and families. The problems of latch-key children, truancy and juvenile crimes are already grave. Family life is sweet, and it must be a matter of personal choice at what age and how much a mother leaves her children.' (McCowan 1975 : 23)

In this structural and cultural context, for women to move from the world of the family to that of politics remains a radical step. In this context, too, it is fully understandable why women have moved in the largest numbers into less prestigious and influential areas, at levels with the lowest amounts of power and authority. In such positions they experience less conflict between family and public commitments, they face less competition and less discrimination: in short, they present the least challenge to the traditional gender order.

In her study of Gislea, an isolated village of the Fens, Mary Chamberlain (1977) writes that most women see little point in taking an interest in politics. The village remains rigidly hierarchical in its attitudes and there are few life options for women apart from marriage and caring for a family. But women have always taken an interest in local affairs and for some this has now been extended to parish council work. One result is that the 'women parish councillors do not consider themselves politically motivated or active in their work' (1977 : 131). They view it as an extension of their general interest in village affairs, closely associated with their involvement in other local organizations, especially the Women's Institute.

One of the contributors to Chamberlain's oral history, Elizabeth Thurston, herself the first woman to be elected to the council, felt that ' "politics doesn't enter into it at all. . . . People voted for councillors for what they are, what they know them to be, not what they might be, or what they might stand for" ' (Chamberlain 1977 : 137). Her activism was prompted by an interest in local affairs; as she put it, ' "I joined the Council because I'm a bit nosey. I like to know what's going on" ' (p. 137). She felt that local unlike national politics was something she could identify with and understand: ' "local government, that's something I can visualise. It's no good talking to me about something I have no idea about. But if it's something concrete, that I know where it is or what it is, then it interests me" ' (1977 : 136).

While an interest in local politics was central to both their lives, neither Elizabeth Thurston nor her sole woman companion on the parish council, Eileen Woolnough, had further political ambitions. They clearly felt that women like themselves have no place in 'politics proper'. As Elizabeth Thurston put it, ' "I would never stand as Member of Parliament – that's beyond me" ' (1977 : 136). Even at the local level, neither woman felt she was equipped, at least in the foreseeable future, to stand as council chairman.

Eileen Woolnough said: ' "I don't want to go any further than this level in politics – I could never stand for chairman or anything like that. Our present one is very, very good. He's re-elected each time. But you have to know a lot more than I do to be chairman" ' (1977 : 140).

It is clear that women in Gislea did not feel confident enough to challenge the male hegemony in the public domain; indeed, they did not aspire to political equality with men. They felt they had an important contribution to make, one which was unlike that of the men. In Elizabeth Thurston's view, most village women were too tied up with home and family to take an interest in politics. And Eileen Woolnough felt that although there is a place for women in local government, it is a secondary one: ' "I don't think you've got to get too many women on the Council. I didn't ought to say this, perhaps, but women do tend to go on a bit over some things, so I don't think you want too many" ' (1977 : 140).

So who are the women who succeed?

We saw at the outset (p. 92) that the first women MPs were surrogates for their men. Is success in the public domain still a matter of either having a supportive family or denying the traditional role of women and remaining single and not having children whether married or not? This still seems to be the case to quite a considerable extent. A decreasing proportion of women in the fifty years since the flapper vote have entered Parliament as substitutes for men (what Currell (1974) called 'male equivalence'). Of the twenty-five women first elected in the period 1929 to 1944, six fall in this category, but there have only been one or two since the end of the Second World War. The practice continues, Currell suggests, in giving Life Peerages to the widows of men who have been active in public life, or including them in the Honours List. She mentions the widows of a former Prime Minister, two eminent politicians, a general secretary of the Labour party. One could also mention the recent elevation of the widow of Airey Neave after he was assassinated while in office. Currell notes also that women office-holders in the Conservative party have often been the widows of the party's male elite (Currell 1974 : 169).

Political families

Men as well as women wishing to make a public career are encouraged by being brought up in politically active families. Currell and Vallance both draw attention to the extent to which women MPs have benefited from this, although there was no

156

data to compare the importance of this factor between men and women. A political career is something well understood by a woman reared in a politically active family and her vision of what is possible for her will be quite different from that of a woman brought up in a non-political family. Currell refers to 'politicized families', like the Churchills, the Devonshires, and the Salisburys, who have a strong tradition of leadership and civic responsibility (Currell 1974 : 164; Vallance 1979 : 61–3).

Most women in such families remain in the background supporting their fathers and husbands and making important connections by marriage between members of these dynasties. In their study of the social background and connections of 'Top Decision Makers' (including Ministers, senior civil servants, and directors of financial and commercial enterprises) Lupton and Wilson (1973) do not mention either in their diagrams or their text the names of the linking women. The women are clearly central to their theme but remain 'hidden from history', essential to the success of their fathers, husbands, and sons: but they have no position of their own in the public world, their existence is not even recorded.

But some women from such families do enter the House. Currell reports that of the thirty-two Labour and twenty-one Conservative MPs first elected to Parliament in the period 1945 to 1970, 47 per cent of the Labour members and 43 per cent of the Conservatives 'could be traced as having, or having had members of their (extended) family active in politics locally or nationally' (1974 : 69). Speaking of the 1974–79 Parliament, Vallance refers to Gwyneth Dunwoody, the daughter of Morgan Phillips, a former Labour Party General Secretary; Shirley Summerskill, the daughter of Edith Summerskill; to those from politically aware families, like Shirley Williams, Barbara Castle, Betty Harvie Anderson, Lynda Chalker, Margaret Thatcher, Joan Lestor, Joan Maynard and Ann Taylor, Audrey Wise and Maureen Colquhoun. Other women MPs told of unusually high political consciousness or sense of public responsibility in their families of origin (Vallance 1979 : 61–4).

Both Currell and Vallance agree that the importance of coming from a political family may be relatively greater for a woman than for a man, because of the strong weight of tradition against

157

women entering politics. Being brought up in a political family will encourage a sense of personal and political efficacy (Currell 1974 : 164, 166; Vallance 1979 : 63). This does not imply, however, that the women will necessarily follow their family's or father's political opinion.

> 'Susan Lawrence (Lab) . . . was brought up in a strongly Conservative family and started her own political life as a Conservative councillor. Joan Lestor (Lab) . . . says she owes her original political education to a father whose views were well to the left of the Labour Party, while Oonagh McDonald's family were, she says, Liberals.' (Vallance 1979 : 62)

This suggests that although their family base was important, these women have struck out on their own in their public lives.

Supportive families

Vallance reports that many of the women MPs she talked to 'stressed the importance of co-operative families – particularly supportive husbands' (Vallance 1979 : 67). This is particularly the case where a woman MP is a wife and mother. The hours of the House, from mid-afternoon until any time of the night, suit lawyers better than housewives. Some marriages survive a shared political commitment, others do not. Vallance implies that not only are supportive husbands seen as essential to political success, but also that they are relatively unusual since most men do not wish to be outshone by their wives. She attributes part of Mrs Thatcher's success to having an older husband 'who had come to the end of his own successful career just at the point where Mrs Thatcher's star was in the ascendant' (Vallance 1979 : 69). There was no marital competition therefore.

Avoiding family commitments

Currell found that in her sample there was a relatively high proportion of single women, childless wives, and widows; the problems of combining home and work were thus minimized. However the decline that Currell reports in the number of married women standing for Parliament did not seem to be the case for 1977. Vallance found that there has been a progressive decline in the number of women MPs who are married from 75 per cent in 1945 to 56 per cent in February 1974, and 59 per cent in the October election of that year (Vallance 1979 : 66). The percentage in the present House of those who are or have been married is 68 per cent. Finkelstein in interviewing American women executives found that 'a disproportionate number . . . have never been married or are divorced, and that a few are lesbian' (Finkelstein 1980 : 194). Mackie and Pattullo suggest that such has been the case at least until relatively recently in Britain (1977 : 73).

Upper- and middle-class women

Those women who come from wealthy families are also more likely to be able to get support in their domestic roles. Currell reports, and this is confirmed by Vallance (1979), that a disproportionate number of women MPs come from the upper and middle classes in the period she studied, as they did in the first ten years following enfranchisement. Working-class women in the House have been unmarried or childless (Margaret Bondfield is an early example) (Vallance 1979 : 38). Mrs Thatcher had a nanny for her twins (Vallance 1979 : 69). Although Vallance reports a decline in the number of married women in the House, she also reports an increase in the 1974 Parliament of women with children: 1950, seven women (33 per cent); October 1974, fifteen women (55 per cent). Most of the children are grown up but it is a sign that times might be changing, that although Helene Hayman's political career is undoubtedly helped by having a nanny, she took a stand about feeding her baby in the 'public arena' of the House. This increasing confidence of women will be referred to later.

Higher education and professional occupations

In addition to coming from upper-middle-class families, successful political women tend to have come above averagely from among the better-educated. We saw earlier (p. 98) that this feature had already begun to emerge in the thirties. Currell shows in the period 1945 to 1970 38 per cent of Conservative women and

159

45 per cent of Labour women were graduates (Currell 1974 : 67). In 1974 63 per cent of women MPs had degrees (Vallance 1979 : 64). While both men and women MPs are more highly educated than average, this is especially true, proportionately, for the women.

Currell has pointed out that there tends to be a concentration in the background of women MPs of 'occupations which involve interaction with people, the skills and techniques of speech and the written word, the formulation and exchange of ideas. Such occupations include all kinds of teaching, the legal profession, public relations, journalism' (Currell 1974 : 56–7). These occupations all contain a high component of what Currell calls a 'communication factor', and involve many of the skills and techniques of value in a political career. This applied to 70 per cent of Labour women and half of the Conservative women from 1945–70.

Of the thirty-seven non-incumbent women Labour candidates in the 1979 General Election, six were lecturers, nine teachers, four researchers, three trade union officers, two lawyers, one accountant, and four members of the 'caring professions'. Of the six classified as housewives all but two were university trained (Labour Party 1979 : 2). At the same time Vallance has pointed out that women, once elected, tend to become 'professional politicians' and to concentrate solely on their political career, not linking, for example, law and politics or indeed other activities as so many men members do (Vallance 1979 : 111). In any case of course, as we have already seen (p. 138), women are a tiny minority in all the more prestigious professions.

The success factors summarized

Women who are successful in political careers tend therefore to come from middle- and upper-class backgrounds and from professional occupations; they have been able to rely on the resources and support of their families or to have minimized the handicaps deriving from women's status within the family by remaining unmarried or childless or by entering public life later in life when their familial obligations have, to a larger degree, been completed.

Failure to apply or refusal of entry?

We must not underestimate the extent to which the present sex-imbalances in positions of power, prestige, and influence are the result of institutional arrangements outside the particular institutions in which the persistence of traditional gender roles are found. There are the sex-role stereotyping of girls at home before school, in school, at the undergraduate level so that they fail to proceed to post-graduate work; the assumption that the child-bearer is the child-rearer; the failure to provide adequate nursery accommodation, and so on. The result is that even those who are prepared to discriminate positively in favour of women (or more cynically to look for a token woman) may have real difficulty in finding persons qualified, willing, and able to be appointed.

> 'Whatever reasons may be adduced for the very low involve-
> ment of women in national politics, the fundamental one still
> has to be that very few women come forward. Most of the MPs
> I interviewed made the point one way or another that women
> do not think in terms of doing this kind of job, yet they said it
> is quite possible for a woman with enough incentive to do it.'
> (Vallance 1979 : 60)

It is clear from her work, from that of Currell, and from the accounts provided by political women themselves that women have to make more effort than men to succeed, to be in some sense better, or at least keener. We have discussed the ideological assumption that politics is not a place for women, which must of itself reduce the number of women coming forward; we have discussed the difficulties of child-rearing and politicking at one and the same time. What other problems do aspiring women members of the House have to cope with? After all, central party organizations have called for more women to put themselves forward as candidates. Do they experience difficulty in obtaining sponsors? In the Labour Party, trade union support may not be readily forthcoming, and we have indicated women's general lack of public bases of power. But, having put themselves forward, do women experience discrimination at selection? Does this put others off? The answer to the first question has to be yes and no. Work by Brookes (1967), Rush (1969), and Currell (1974) suggest that the smaller number of women selected by the Conservative party in relation to the number of candidates may be evidence that women seeking selection by local Conservative parties may not get a fair hearing. Vallance's (1979) study leads her to the view that while it is fairly easy to get on a short-list in both parties, because the local parties wish to be seen to be encouraging women candidates in line with national party policy, women may not subsequently be treated equally with men candidates (Vallance 1979 : 46–7). With regard to the selection of candidates for the Labour Party in 1976–77, of the total number of people nominated, 10 per cent were women; of the total short-listed, 11 per cent; of the total selected, 13 per cent were women. This might look like positive discrimination until one discovers that women tend not to be selected for the better seats. As Jill Hills puts it, Labour women candidates 'may have a better than even chance of being selected, but for safe Conservative seats'(Hills n.d. : 15). The situation had not changed from when Pamela Brookes wrote:

> 'it has not been really difficult for a woman of good qualifications and sufficient determination to find a seat to contest, provided she is willing to take on a constituency that has little chance of returning her. The real hurdle is to get adopted for a winnable seat.' (1967 : 243)

It is not surprising that party selectorates reflect and reinforce the attitudes, beliefs, and values about the role of women in politics that are widespread throughout society. This is Rush's view about the failure of the Conservative Party to select more women candidates. Rush refers first to 'adherence to the rather vague notion that being an MP or candidate, especially the former, is a man's job' (1969 : 64). It is assumed that women are not qualified to do this job. Women have experience only of marriage and housewifery. Men have successful careers in business and the professions. We have shown above that this is not merely prejudice. It *is* the case in our society that women's position in the family is rarely irrelevant to their position in the public world. The successful political women are those who can minimize this 'family effect' as well as developing other skills. As Rush says:

162

'Single women are far more likely to fulfil the conditions of a successful career, and, moreover, do not have the family commitments of married women' (1969 : 64). Thus, single women are also looked upon more favourably in the selection process and are more likely to put themselves forward as potential candidates.

The second factor, according to Rush, is a 'general preference for married men' (1969 : 64). Once again, common social attitudes are involved. The advantage of the married man is simply that he has a wife who 'is expected to be an asset to the association and to the constituency. She must support her husband on the platform' (1969 : 65). As well as performing works of charity, looking after the needs of the sick and the young, and gracing social gatherings with her presence, she may also be expected to deputize for her husband at those functions 'which he cannot or will not attend' (1969 : 65). There is one more reason for the unpopularity of the married woman candidate. What woman could expect such support from her husband? The public duties of the MP's wife are, in short, not a denial of but an extension of her marital role. Yet, ten years later, Vallance reports that increasingly few male MPs can expect the undistracted services of a wife as more married women pursue careers in their own right (1979 : 67).

Vallance reports that: 'Few of the women members I talked to . . . claimed to be aware of discrimination at the selection stage' (Vallance 1979 : 47) although Labour women were more likely to suspect discrimination than were Conservatives (1979 : 48). Vallance concludes that rather than discrimination it is a question of 'an often unconscious sexism' (1979 : 49) which sees women as inappropriate for politics: the grounds have shifted since the sixties, she thinks, from 'a general rejection of women as women . . . to a rather more secular questioning of their suitability given their female characteristics' (1979 : 48). We are nevertheless back to physical weakness, inappropriate female characteristics, the old familiar list of justifications for women's unsuitability for politics. Vallance reports that having women on selection committees does not necessarily help women candidates. Many women MPs reported to her that much of their most hostile questioning and underlining of the importance of woman's role as wife and mother came from the women selectors: women who have accepted a traditional and home-bound domestic role are not always or perhaps not often sympathetic to the liberation of others.

At other levels of political activity, which may be seen as more appropriate for women, the outcome may be different and women's support of women candidates may be of the essence. Elizabeth Thurston of Gislea was sure she would not have been elected to the parish council but for the support of women (she was President of the Women's Institute at the time). ' "I think the women voted for me because they knew that possibly if something came up that they wanted a woman to fight for, I would fight for them" ' (Chamberlain 1975 : 137). This then was her power base and as both she and Mrs Woolnough recognized, the experience of public speaking and of handling meetings, which they had gained in the Institute, was an important factor in their decision to try for the Council.

At the Parliamentary level, suitably qualified and experienced women candidates may be ignored. Maureen Colquhoun has observed in relation to public appointments, ' "when it comes to appointing women to public organizations they are not merely regarded as second class citizens but in some cases it seems, their very existence has been completely overlooked" ' (quoted in Mackie and Pattullo 1977 : 92). Such actions occur against a background of common sense which stresses the importance of family life and claims to recognize the value of women's contribution. At the same time, the work that women carry out for their families is trivialized, considered 'unskilled' and not suitable as a qualification for public responsibility, so that any possible contribution women might make to public life is called into question.

There is no evidence to suggest that women candidates' lower chances of success are attributable to 'voter resistance' to women (Currell 1974; Goot and Reid 1975; Newland 1975). It is generally agreed that the sex of the candidate is irrelevant to the vast majority of voters: 'on the day of the election it is the party that counts' (Ross 1955 : 266). But such evidence may not weigh heavy on the day of selection. 'When it comes down to it, a constituency is choosing a single individual and is less likely to opt for an outsider. A woman, given both the general and specifically political image of women, is an outsider and is disadvantaged accordingly' (Vallance 1979 : 51). Thus, while equality between the sexes is accepted as a general abstract principle, political sponsors so often decide, especially when the stakes are high, that selecting a man presents the 'safest' alternative.

The political work women are expected to do

The Gislea women were clear that women have a special and separate contribution to make to parish affairs. Mrs Thurston believed that women ' "tend to see things differently to men – a different point of view and sometimes a more practical point of view than a man" ' (Chamberlain 1975 : 135–36). Mrs Woolnough agreed, ' "I think it's a good thing we're on it. I think the women want somebody on there to represent them" ' (1975 : 140).

Elizabeth Thurston saw her role as fighting to get things done for women and especially children. Backed by the Women's Institute, the women parish councillors had taken a leading part in a campaign for a 'school' sign in the village. In this way they were allowed and even expected to express concern over matters connected with the traditional task of women as wives and mothers. There was even some doubt, at least in Elizabeth Thurston's mind, whether women would be said to have any other interests at all: ' "you can't really say that there's anything specifically for women – you tend to think of it as for families. You tend to look after the children" .' (Chamberlain 1975 : 137).

These attitudes are echoed at the national level. Edward Heath, when asked whether he would like to see more women in politics, replied, ' "Yes, I would, in the House of Commons and outside it at all levels, so long as they are providing what women can, and not just duplicating what men can do, which probably would lead to them not making a woman's contribution anyway" ' (Brookes 1967 : 267).

The vision of women in positions of public authority remains difficult to reconcile with conventional ideas of proper womanly conduct. Reconciliation is easier to the extent that women's political activities can still be linked to their traditional role. Women are therefore allowed and expected to specialize in

165

'women's affairs'. It is not only that women are to be found more often in the less prestigious and influential political bodies, it is also true that the nearer the concerns of an organization or assembly to women's traditional sphere, the more women we find there. This is an area, however, where as we shall see some women determine to take a stand. At the local and national levels in Britain, women are found in greatest numbers in areas concerned with family, educational, and health affairs rather than with defence, fiscal policy, or employment. Women MPs have tended to promote, but more importantly have been expected to promote, Private Members' Bills on questions of moral or family welfare, to 'put the woman's point of view'.

But 'women's subjects' are 'low in prestige and often regarded as marginal or relatively unimportant in government activity' (Rendel 1977 : 7). Betsy Thom has confirmed this tendency for international organizations. There, as in national elites, women in higher positions are found in the organization's 'periphery', 'in cultural and "women's affairs" rather than in the centre, and in the advisory rather than the decision-making spheres' (Thom 1980 : 171). In the United Nations women accounted for only 4.3 per cent to 7.5 per cent of the total membership in six of the seven main committees, but for 23 per cent of the Social Humanitarian and Cultural Committee – 'the dumping ground for so-called "women's problems" ' (1980 : 171). Significantly, the first woman Assistant General Secretary was appointed to Social Development and Humanitarian Affairs.

Similarly, Chaney argues for the Latin American case that women are to be found in those posts and departments which are traditionally considered to be women's affairs and furthest away from concern with socio-economic development or change. Almost 75 per cent of the women office-holders in her sample held positions that they and others viewed as extensions of their traditional role. The women had a distinct style of political role performance:

> 'The woman official often sees herself as a kind of *supermadre* in the large *casa* of the municipality and even the nation, where she views her work as differing only in magnitude from the nurturant and affectional tasks women perform for husband and family.' (Chaney 1973 : 104)

166

If women are expected to specialize in women's affairs, this does not mean that men are excluded from the higher levels in such fields. We have already seen that men tend to take over managerial and policy-making positions even in areas in which women have traditionally predominated. In UNICEF in 1974 no woman professional was apparently worthy of a directional grade – even in a field closely associated with her traditional concerns. 'It must be really hard', Betsy Thom comments, 'to find a woman who has some expertise in matters of child care, health, education, and nutrition' (Thom 1980 : 178). In one very important sense it is difficult to find a woman since 'expertise' and management skills have been defined as male prerogatives: women's skills in these areas have been expropriated by professionals. Other 'woman's affairs', such as fertility control, are apparently the prerogative of men. In such areas women have fought to become involved, of which more later. Often, however, to be consulted is no more than the right to put their point of view *to the experts*, as the following plea for more women to enter local government clearly shows:

> '(Women) have a vested interest in, and immediate knowledge of, the schools, services, housing, care of children and the environment which are the responsibility of the local authorities. They should not feel that they have nothing to offer but commonsense and a desire 'to get things done', since professional experts advise every committee, and these are the very qualities needed.' (McCowan 1975 : 18)

There was a reaction against this relegation to 'women's affairs' (see Rendel 1977 : 7). Barbara Castle, for example, all through her political life has wished 'to be accepted as a competent *person* with political interests which were not in the least dictated by her feminine experience' (Vallance 1979 : 85, emphasis in original). She recalled to Elizabeth Vallance her own strong resentment, when she was in local government before the Second World War, of a move to put her on the committee on maternity and child welfare on the basis that she was a woman. She was much more interested in transport and industry than in consumerism or education which she resisted taking. Similarly, Judith Hart thought 'that it was only by tackling the areas beyond those

167

traditionally assigned to women that she could establish herself as a credible politician' (Vallance 1979 : 85). Harold Wilson while Prime Minister played an innovative part in breaking the traditional pattern, including appointing Barbara Castle as Minister of Transport, Judith Hart as Paymaster General, and Eirene White as Parliamentary Secretary to the Colonial Office (see Vallance 1979 : 36, 85). Margaret Thatcher, despite her own unconventional career, has sadly not maintained this initiative.

Separate organization?

Associated with this debate is the question of separate women's organizations within the political parties and the TUC. Both major parties have their women's organizations, which service the party machines. In the Labour Party and the TUC the matter has been seriously debated. There are those who feel that the existence of separate organizations makes it possible for women to learn about politics, to speak and debate, and to thrash out women's affairs. Others argue that such separate organization reinforces the tendency of the male-dominated parties to see women's issues as trivial, secondary, and removable to another and powerless forum. In both the Labour Party and the TUC the consensus has been that the time is not yet ripe to give up a form of organization that recognizes, albeit inadequately, women's general under-representation in the movement as a whole. Women had initially to assert a right to organize in their own interests. They have now to judge the strategy by which they can most effectively modify the agenda determined by the men in the public domain.

The development of a consciousness of women for women

Women MPs 'fight shy of "women's issues" in order to keep their place in a man's world' (Mitchell 1971 : 132), because masculine standards are taken as the criterion of success and in this man's world 'women's issues' are at the bottom of the political agenda. We have seen (Chapter 5) that the party political divisions already existing between the men in the public domain, associated as they were with deep-seated class divisions between women as well as men, prevented the formation of a woman's party. Sympathy has always been reported as existing between women MPs despite party differences, and this is not surprising given their tiny minority in the House.

There is still no suggestion of a woman's party developing, but there are signs of change in the public stance of political women. Actions which one generation felt necessary are felt less necessary by a later generation. Thus Vallance reports that Dr Edith Summerskill insisted on retaining her maiden name, which was then later taken by her children, while Helene Middleweek decided to become Mrs Hayman upon marriage, although there is no doubt at all of her sympathy with feminist issues (Vallance 1979 : 114–15). She felt sufficiently confident that she would still be treated as a woman in her own right.

Vallance also describes interestingly the growing awareness in the 1974–79 House among the women members of their common womanhood, and their greatly increased self-confidence as women which has led them to challenge a male-dominated agenda order *in the interests of women*. This new spirit arose particularly with regard to the abortion bill. Fertility control, as we remarked earlier, has in the past been defined as a male prerogative: the intervention of James White, then William Benyon, and subsequently John Corrie galvanized many women's organizations in the country into action to preserve the relatively liberal 1967 Abortion Act. Vallance reports how it was left to the women in the House to organize the opposition in the 1974–79 Parliament, to organize and to work hard to defeat the bills. The final defeat of the Corrie bill in 1980 against all predictable odds is a further indication of the organizational sophistication and determination of women as women. Vallance argues that the Abortion Debate (1974–77)

> 'symbolized the wider demand by women that their ideas and priorities should be taken as they were presented and neither defined by men, nor distorted by being presented as seen through the lenses of male opinion. . . . Women, as Mrs Hayman put it, no longer want to be surrogate men.' (Vallance 1979 : 93)

There emerges a clear distinction between the older women who

169

fought for a place in a man's world for themselves, and a younger generation, influenced by the women's liberation movement, who wish to change that world so that it is as much a women's as a man's world. That day seems yet far off, but there have undoubtedly been significant changes in attitudes, behaviour, and consciousness since the vote was won. Given the odds, we still think the achievement in such a short time has been remarkable.

EIGHT

Conclusions: given the odds, a great advance

'It may well be that there are many women today who do not appreciate what a race has been run in the past hundred years, and at what cost it was run by those who were pioneers. . . . It is because of the battles fought and won in the past – forcing open the doors of education and the professions, winning the right to vote – that it is possible to place on today's agenda the next steps which are necessary to force open the doors still wider and make further advances on the road to women's equality.' (Ramelson 1972 : 53 and 188)

'Traditionally, the interior, private world of the home is feminine and thus the integration of women into the public world of work and industry is only partial. The contradiction which appears clearly in capitalism between family and industry, private and public, personal and impersonal, is the fissure in women's consciousness through which revolt erupts. The clash between the mass scale of commodity production and the micro-unit of the family and intimate sexual fantasy is thus the moment of women's liberation. But the questions that come out . . . are of significance not only for women. . . . How can we connect to our everyday living the commitment to make a society without exploitation and oppression? What is the relationship between the objective changes in capital-ism and our new perceptions of social revolution? What are the ways in which we can organize together without sacrificing our autonomy?' (Rowbotham 1973 : xv–xvi)

The limited advances made

As we conclude this book the first woman Prime Minister heads the British government. She has no other woman in her cabinet and stands out as an 'exceptional woman' (Mitchell 1971 : 129). Mrs Thatcher's leadership alone among twenty-two men perhaps symbolizes the paradox that has been a theme throughout: how few women there are in positions of power, and yet how far women have come in a short space of time. We can appreciate the views of Ramelson (1972 : 53) quoted at the head of this chapter. As a communist-feminist of long standing, she wrote in the mid-sixties, when she herself was about sixty, that many women do not appreciate the advances that have been made. At the same time we also share the strongly expressed feelings of younger feminists who experience their own and their sisters' continued oppression.

In this book we have argued on two grounds that it is surprising how far women have come in their attempts to enter the public domain and the political arena which lies in that domain. The first is that women had never before the seventeenth century attempted to act as individuals in their own right rather than as members of families. It was not until the twentieth century that they were accorded some, but still not all, of the civil rights which would give them equality with men to act as persons. Our second main ground was based on the empirical fact that no significant alterations were made in the institution of the family nor in the traditional division of labour. Equality before the law for men made possible the development of a profoundly class-divided capitalist society (Marshall 1963; Mitchell 1976). Equal-

172

ity was mocked in practice. The form of the family under advanced capitalism and the welfare state has similarly mocked equality for women. We have also argued that in attempting to move into the public domain women are not only faced with the opposition of the majority of men, but that the resources which women can command and the oppression which they suffer varies from one class to another and from fraction to fraction within a class. The entry of women into education proved important but insufficient; Wollstonecraft and successive feminists in the nineteenth century who argued for it had good reason. Education has been one of the few resources that women have been able to use to free themselves from the constraints of the traditional role. Providing both sexes with routes for upward mobility in a changing society, education has made it possible for women to stand alongside and against men in the public political arena, and this notwithstanding that educational opportunities are not really anywhere near equal between the sexes (Deem 1978; Wolpe 1978); nor, of course, are these opportunities equal among the classes.

Varieties of power

We have found it necessary to disaggregate the nature of the oppression of women and to distinguish various forms of power. Women may be profoundly inferior, as in Muslim society, but still exercise power not only within the family or kin group, but from that position beyond into the public domain. We are interested to note that in discussing the political participation of women in Latin America, Jaquette (1976) warns that by accepting Western strategies women may lose the power that they can now exercise as wives and mothers and through their associated communication networks. They have a powerful private domain; better perhaps to continue to use it, especially as studies have shown that women lose power in urbanization and industrialization.

We have seen that women in twentieth-century Western societies may have apparent equality but lack power in the private domain and have very few ways of taking part in the public domain. Acceptance as persons in their own right in the Western

173

world has not brought to women an equal share of the power, or even a considerable share. In politics the situation of women is worse in numerical terms in Britain now, despite there being a woman prime minister, than it was when we started writing. Furthermore, and ironically, the government is acting against those very slender social supports that survived the Second World War to help to modify the unequal division of labour in the family: nurseries and nursery schools are prime targets for government cuts. The vote has not modified government policy in favour of women in the way that the nineteenth- and early twentieth-century feminists had hoped it would.

Contemporary feminists' lack of emphasis on formal political power

In contrast to the suffragette movement, the latter-day feminist movement has paid little attention to politics in the sense of being involved in attempts to seize formal political power for women. Politics for the women's liberation movement has been seen as a direct struggle with men in everyday life and of campaigning for specific improvements in state legislation or provision: campaigns for nurseries, the right to chose whether to have an abortion, the provision of free contraception, the exposure of violence in the family, and direct attention to help battered wives. The failure to engage with formal political power arose largely because women's liberation came out of the anarcho-libertarian ethos of the late 1960s.* That movement rejected established societies which were seen as repressive and rejected also all their associated institutions and values. Part at least of the women's liberation movement shared these views. They are expressed in a strong form by James, who sees a clear division between being 'political' and being feminist. 'Political' women compromise with men and with the capitalist state, feminists must develop new forms of politics inherent in the autonomy of women (James 1972). Vallance reports the division among the organizers of a fund-raising meeting for the Working Women's

* I am indebted to discussion with Jalna Hanmer for clarification of these issues. M.S.

174

Charter held at Alexandra Palace in 1977 as to whether a woman should open it. 'One faction claimed that women in Parliament were part of the male establishment while the other saw benefits in the support a well-known woman would attract' (1979 : 113).

Alternatives

For all those feminists who take an anarcho-libertarian viewpoint, to strive for formal political power is seen as condoning a repressive society. Incorporation or 'co-option' was to be avoided at all costs. The aim was to develop alternative life styles. It was one of the great contributions of the anarcho-libertarian movement that it gave rise to mutually supportive and caring groups. It was a sorrow that in so many of the communes which were associated with a part of it men continued to dominate and exploit women (Rigby 1974; Abrams and McCulloch 1976).

As Abrams and McCulloch have shown, while the communes were set up among other reasons because of a general dissatisfaction with the nuclear family 'few if any communes were explicitly concerned with "the woman question"' (1976 : 5). There was the notion that in communes women would live as individuals in their own right.

> 'More substantially perhaps, communal living was seen as possibly realising a blueprint drawn by Engels: "With the passage of the means of production into common property, the individual family ceases to be the economic unit of society. Private housekeeping is transformed into social industry. The care and education of the children becomes a public matter".'
> (Abrams and McCulloch 1976 : 5)

In practice unsupported mothers often turned to communes as a solution for their problems. Abrams and McCulloch were themselves interested in the possibility that in communes the social process of mothering might be separated from the exploitation of biological mothers. In practice they found that this did not come about. 'Of the three links that compose the basic family unit, wife-husband, father-child, mother-child, the first two are often seriously opened up in communes, but the third is hardly touched; motherhood remains an all-demanding and totally female role' (Abrams and McCulloch 1976 : 144). Women in communes have not achieved liberation. Indeed, there is a sense in which they are more exploitable, woman poses as the equal of man 'without the strength of real equality to defend herself' (1976 : 144). Women worry constantly in the commune, as they do outside: 'What shall I do if he leaves me?' (1976 : 145). Abrams and McCulloch see communes as the reconstitution of familism in which the removal of legally-enforceable monogamy and the wage-work-housework division of roles has not created an alternative system but 'the deeper obstacles to equality through which men in this society struggle to relate are made plainer' (1976 : 145).

A major reason for this is in their view derived from the basic individualism that lay behind the commune movement, which they see as a form of petty-bourgeois protest. The issue essentially was one of the emancipation of the individual 'that is emancipation *from* social relations rather than *through* social relations' (1976 : 141, emphasis in original). In addition the pressures of the outside capitalist world bear upon and constrain relations within the commune in a variety of ways. For the women this is mediated by the schools to which the children are sent and from which they return with demands for 'normal parents'. The man can assert his freedom, so the woman offers herself as a 'normal parent' partially to meet this demand and in defence of her child. It is capitalist society that Abrams and McCulloch see as impinging on and preventing the liberation of women: 'Once the involvement of personal relationships in a wage labour economy has been broken, sexual inequality at the level of personal relations is neither plausible nor necessary' (1976 : 132). It is not sufficient to attempt to live in an enclave within capitalist society, an enclave which cannot avoid interaction with members and institutions of that society.

This is similar to the point which Caulfield (1977 : 60–77) makes about the denigration of use values in capitalist society. She draws on works (especially those of Leacock (1975) and Godelier (1975)) which analyse societies where there is no clear division between the public and private domain and upon Marx's notion of 'use value' as opposed to 'exchange value'. Exchange

176

occurs in societies based on use value, but is based on generalized reciprocity rather than exact equivalence: 'all producers give to the group, thus making a material and spiritual bond between themselves and the total group, affirming overall solidarity, survival, and their own belongingness' (Caulfield 1977 : 74). These values are lost in societies such as capitalist societies which are based on exchange values. Use value survives in small pockets, as in housework, but it is denigrated in consequence of the dominant exchange values. This accounts for the dislike of housework reported by Oakley for example (see pp. 122–25 above). What is valued is not intrinsic to the nature of the task but is determined by the dominant social relations. Thus did the communes find difficulty in asserting and maintaining their values and their preferred social relations surrounded as they were by the values and the relationships of capitalist society.

Experiences with male domination in communes was one of the reasons why many women both here and in the US came to conclude, correctly in our view, that it is not only the capitalist mode of production which has to be overcome before women can be liberated, but the male-dominated society, whether or not one agrees with Marcuse that all domination is patriarchal domination (1979). It would seem that if the removal of a wage labour economy is a necessary condition for liberation, it is not a sufficient condition. Relations of domination and subordination in the family and the kin group have occurred for many millennia and are a form of social relations which are not directly consequent upon capitalism: indeed in a capitalist society it is the *unwaged* nature of women's work in the patriarchal family that constitutes a major part of her exploitation. Some women, in the face of male exploitation, have indeed decided that the main thrust of the struggle must be to overthrow patriarchy: hence the major division between the radical feminists and the socialist feminists, a dispute as to the part played by capitalism in woman's oppression. (See Nelson and Olesen (1977) for a useful overview; Hamilton (1978) for a stimulating theoretical discussion; and Weinbaum (1978); Beechey (1979) helpfully disentangles the various meanings of patriarchy.)

Some women, recognizing the continued power of men, therefore pursue a policy of living and working together to overthrow patriarchy. Hence the importance of the lesbian movement within contemporary women's liberation in Britain today (Ettore 1980). It is not just that homosexual women have turned to the movement which can offer them support in an otherwise unsympathetic and hostile society, although that is part of it. It is that women in the radical wing of the movement, some initially heterosexual, have consciously decided to adopt a homosexual life style for political reasons. Others have decided to remain celibate. Only by not admitting the enemy to bed, they believe, can patriarchy be overthrown. This position has its problems. As Beechey has pointed out: 'It is unclear what the revolutionary feminists' conception of the non-patriarchal society would be and how such a society would reproduce itself' (1979 : 70).

Individualism and entry into the public domain

We have argued that the development of individualism and capitalism meant that the bourgeois form of the family, which developed concomitantly, carried within it the seeds of its own destruction. It was inevitable that women, being human, should wish to have applied to themselves the individual rights claimed by the men. In parts of the women's movement, perhaps most obviously in the white middle-class movement in the USA, it is therefore not surprising that most attention has been paid to women's rights, modelled on civil rights. It follows logically in a society dominated by the twin ideologies of individualism and egalitarianism and with a tradition of feminism over 100 years old, that women should demand equal rights with men. Women found themselves frustrated in their attempts to pursue careers and their consciousness of their oppression was raised by the women's movement, which thus gathered further momentum. The long-term implications for the sisterhood of their competitive, striving, upward mobility was not a dominant issue. They formed supportive groups to help each other enter the male world of work and succeed there. The risk of the destruction of their sisterly attachments, and perhaps ultimately the destruction of the sisterhood, which might result from this strategy, was not prominent in their writings. So far as this aspect of their aims for liberation was concerned it was to enter and achieve advancement, hitherto denied women, in the male world of work. This branch of the women's movement in the USA was much more likely to be concerned with the attainment of political power: the political elite was one among a number of elites, all part of the public domain and hitherto dominated by men, which these women wished to enter. For them it was a question of elites, for they were not hampered by a class analysis of society.

In Britain upwardly mobile women have been less closely associated with the latest phase of the feminist movement; the women's liberation movement in Britain is more noticeably dominated by young women than it is in the USA. Our analysis would suggest that in so far as women's goal is to share public power in its present form with men, those women who were demanding equal rights and were concerned with entry into positions of economic power were correct. For those positions would make it possible for them to enter the political arena at the national and international level. But women, as we have seen, have had difficulty in achieving senior positions in capitalist corporations and in trade unions as well as in political parties.

The opposition of men to women's advancement

We have had to conclude that men have been acting as a group, albeit largely or at least partly unconsciously, to restrict the activity of women, and that they have done this because it is in their interests as men, as husbands and fathers, and as employers, administrators, and politicians to keep women as nearly as possible in their traditional place, while at the same time using their labour for production, reproduction, and to increase consumption. Full entry of women into the public domain and a concomitant alteration of the domestic division of labour would, of course, mean that the entire male life-style would have to be altered. As Blood and Wolfe (1960) argue, sharing of tasks in the domestic sphere would reduce specialization in an age of increasing specialization. The entire family life would have to be reorganized. Women entering the public world present a double threat to men: added competition for their jobs and loss of a maintained but unpaid worker in the home. It is certain that many men are quite unaware of their motives or indeed how sexist much of their behaviour is. Their socialization into what is a 'natural' division of labour between the sexes is as deep as that of most women, both seeing the present order as 'natural, right, and proper'. In addition to material interests, many and sophisticated are the ideologies that sustain this view.

All feminists share a rejection of the inevitableness and the rightness of those traditional values, but they vary as to the priorities for action. Neither that part of the women's movement which derived from the anarcho-libertarianism of the sixties nor that part which drew ideas from notions of equality and civil rights have paid much direct attention to the question of women in relation to formal political power. Some socialist-feminist groups in Britain have tried to ensure that women achieve leadership positions in influential intellectual bodies, bodies that can be seen to have a potential for increasing understanding of the nature of male-dominated capitalist society and thus raising the consciousness and will to action of those groups who might be able significantly to modify or overthrow it. But even this policy has proceeded with caution because of the fears of 'co-option'.

Women in Parliament

For all sections of the latter-day women's movement, therefore, the policy of getting women into Parliament has either been deliberately rejected or has taken a secondary place. Yet we made it plain at the end of the last chapter how much all women in Britain owe to the hard work and dedication of those women members of the House who combined to defeat repeated attacks on the 1967 Abortion Act. It has been those women who have followed the tenets of the older feminist movement who have entered Parliament and there fought for equal rights and equal opportunities for women. Nancy Seear was a feminist long before the liberation movement began. Her successful work, along with the Fawcett Society, which survived through the low-key years of feminism, has provided a basis from which women in Britain may fight for more equal opportunities. Some of those things that Marian Ramelson in 1965 saw as requiring a great and organized effort have come about already (Ramelson 1972 : 182). At least, by law women must now be treated as equals with men in pay and promotions. But we know how far the reality deviates from the legal stipulations (see Mackie and Pattullo 1977; Stacey and Price 1979).

The limited value of laws

What has held up the implementation of these laws, we conclude, is the same as the impediments that have restricted the achievements of women in the political arena. None of the other social institutions of society were changed in any radical manner. Most immediately, the social institution of the family and the division of labour within it has remained substantially unchanged. Labour in the family remains an unpaid service provided largely by women for men. This in turn depresses the earning power of women, who can be paid less and encouraged to work part-time and for low pay since they are partially supported by their husbands (cf. Beechey 1977, 1979). The husband is cast in the role of the breadwinner for the family (although in practice we know there are many families with no male breadwinner) and thus passes on to his wife the social relations that he experiences as a wage worker in the public domain. Women being the child-bearers, they continue to be seen as child-rearers, and thus continue to be housewives – still seen as the 'natural' role for women. This notion is backed by apparently scientifically-based evidence that the entry of women into the public domain, at least during the formative years, would be bad for their children (Bowlby 1952).

Feminine characteristics and the political arena

Women and men are perceived and perceive themselves to have different characteristics (see Fransella and Frost 1977). Men are seen as hiding their emotions, being aggressive, independent, objective, dominant, active and competitive, tough and hard. Women, on the other hand, are seen as gentle, tactful, concerned for others, quiet, tender, and caring. These are not qualities which are likely to lead women to want to enter or to be seen to be acceptable in the public domain of competition and struggle for scarce resources; such characteristics, whether exhibited by

181

women or men, belong to the private domain. Margaret Thatcher attracts disapproval, ridicule, and also admiration because she is seen to exhibit some of the stereotypically less well-loved of so-called feminine characteristics and at the same time behaves tough as successful politicians must.

When, in a TV broadcast in 1978 (repeated 21.1.79), Brian Magee asked Herbert Marcuse what new areas ought to be considered by the Frankfurt School, whose scholars were so influential in the 1968 uprisings, Marcuse replied that in his view attention should be paid to the women's liberation movement which he saw as having a strong radical potential. Marcuse was concerned that more attention should be paid to the quality of life under socialism and not just to the material base. The hope he saw flowing from the women's liberation movement was that qualities which have hitherto been specifically feminine, like caring and gentleness, should be diffused through society. As a Marxist he recognized that these specifically feminine qualities are socially conditioned, but nevertheless he argued that the qualities were available, were there and, therefore, should be used.

Feminists have often made the same point. It was to be found in discussions about the vote in the nineteenth and early twentieth centuries and is repeated again today. 'If the women were in power the world would not be in such a mess' or 'We would not have so many wars if the women were in charge.' Part of the discussion at the Kings College conference on Women and Elites (Epstein and Coser 1980) also made the assumption that if women joined the elites, the quality of those elites would change because of the specifically feminine contribution (see also Folsom 1948 : 626–27). This will not happen automatically however. The 'feminine characteristics' are not biologically determined or universally present among womankind, they are closely associated with particular social roles that women have played. In order for the entry of women into the political arena to affect the way politics are played other changes are necessary: the nature of competitive society has also to change, relationships of domination and subordination in the factory and the workplace have to be removed, and men have to become involved in the nurturant roles, that is, the division of labour in the household and family has also to change.

The masculine traits are not inherent: the strength and the toughness come from the training for and experience of the competitive struggle in the public domain of capitalist societies. Women and working-class men have to be taught in their consciousness-raising groups and in their trade union and shop stewards' courses to stand up for themselves and their sisters and brothers. Their inferior social situation has taught them to be subservient and deferential. The feminist movement and the labour movement teach their members to claim equality of status. But those who fight for and enter positions of power in the public world which is dominated by the values of the hierarchical state and exploitative capitalism are very likely, as Hannah Mitchell felt she had been, to be hardened by the struggle (Mitchell 1968 : 191). The gentle and softly yielding woman will not long survive in political battle or in a power position. Sooner or later she will find herself behaving 'like a man' or 'like a boss'.

Tensions in feminism

We saw that there were contradictions inherent in the twin ideologies of individualism and familism which led to the emergence of the bourgeois feminist movement in the seventeenth century. Similarly we saw how these same tensions became implanted in the feminist movement itself and are important within it today. These tensions take two important forms. We saw historically that because nineteenth-century capitalist society was class-divided, the material interests of middle-class and working-class feminists were in conflict despite their common womanhood. We also saw how at one and the same time early feminists wished to achieve autonomy, to retain the affectual ties within the family, and to extend the caring role of women into the political arena.

The problem of the men

There is, in addition, connected with child-bearing but not necessarily connected with child-rearing, the particularly difficult and delicate nature of the struggle for women's emancipation because of the mutual sexuality of women and men. This has also played an important part in holding women back from full entry into the public arena. Sheila Rowbotham (1973) has drawn attention to this difficult and delicate aspect of the struggle of the sexes and how vulnerable the feminists were because they persisted in ignoring the existence of female anatomy. In the two chapters, 'Living Doll' and 'Through the Looking Glass' she describes and analyses her own attempts to come to terms with her sexuality and the relationship of the most intimate connections between men and women to the meaning of women' oppression (Rowbotham 1973 : 12–46). As she argues:

> 'the relationship of man to woman is like no other relationship of oppressor to oppressed. It is far more delicate, far more complex. After all, very often the two love one another. It is rather a gentle tyranny. We are subdued at the very moment of intimacy. Such ecstatic subjugation is thus very different from the relationship between worker and capitalist.' (Rowbotham 1973 : 34–5)

'Consequently', Rowbotham continues, 'the political emergence of women has to be at once distinct from and in connection with men' (1977 : 35).

The problem of equality

In addition to this problem, the tensions associated with equality and class division and with caring roles and values have all to be resolved if women are to go forward to fuller emancipation. The political goals, the strategy and tactics all have to be settled in light of these contradictory indications.

Nelson and Olesen (1977) draw attention to the almost exclusive concentration upon equality in the ideology of contemporary feminist movements. They argue for differentiation, not identicality, as being crucial to selfhood and uniqueness. Their case is an essentially conservative one, which sees differentiation and stratification as inevitable. They fear 'The vision of (an egalitarian) society is the vision of stultifying equilibrium in which personhood so clearly emergent from social differentiation would atrophy' (1977 : 23). They argue, using the case of the Muslim women as evidence (see p. 19), that inequality need not

184

signify inferiority for they believe that a realistic mutuality in relationships can be established notwithstanding differentiation and stratification.

Nelson and Olesen are correct to draw our attention to the failure of the women's movement to make plain what they mean by equality and also to direct our attention to Marxist-feminist anthropologists, such as Eleanor Leacock, for whom egalitarianism 'encompasses the values of inter-relatedness rather than independence, autonomous co-operation rather than aggressive competition, reciprocity and mutuality rather than self-interest and separateness' (Nelson and Olesen 1977 : 32). The problem of the economic and political structure within which such positive values can develop remains. Juliet Mitchell, who accepts the importance of the material basis of class divisions, does not have a vision of 'stultifying equilibrium' when she thinks of a classless society and clearly sees the ideology of equality as an abstract measurement and bound up with class inequalities:

> 'The socialist and communist perspective suggests that "equality" in capitalist societies is based on class inequality; in a classless society there will still be differences or inequalities, inequalities between individuals, strengths or handicaps of various kinds. There will be differences among women and among men; a truly just society based on collective ownership and equal distribution would take these inequalities into account and give more to he who needed more and ask more from he who could give more. This would be a true recognition of the individual in the qualities that are essential to his humanity.' (Mitchell 1976 : 397)

The problem of class

We are dubious whether the theoretical case for the disappearance of sexual oppression when the involvement of personal relationships in a wage economy has been broken has been adequately made. The theory in our view is not yet sufficiently conclusively developed and the ways in which the mode of production and the relations of production of the wider society relate to the production and social relations in the domestic sphere still

185

remain to be satisfactorily worked out. It is clear to us, however, that there are important connections between these arenas. We therefore share Caulfield's view:

> 'Rather than seeking to isolate sex and gender from analysis of the mode of production, we need to integrate the two, and get down to the difficult task of concrete historical materialist studies which will help us to see how differing relations of production, here and in other societies, embody differing forms of sex and gender systems.' (Caulfield 1977 : 66)

The values of mutuality and caring

One of the hazards we see in the entry of women into the public domain, so long as the aggressive competitive society remains, is that those consequences of the present gender divisions which do have value may get lost. We have no illusions about the extent of violence in the family and of the oppressiveness which may enter male-female and parent-child relations in the present system (see, for example, Borland (1976)). But the values of tenderness and caring are present and are permissible in the family more than elsewhere. Caulfield is under no illusions about the denigration of housework, as we mentioned earlier (p. 177). Nevertheless, there are some compensations: 'The unity of doing, thinking and feeling, all expressed in the act of working and giving in a solidary, intimate social group is . . . the essence of use value production' (1977 : 74). But full expression cannot be given to these positive aspects of use value in a predominantly capitalist society. Caulfield writes: 'From personal experience of full-time housework and rearing five children I know that the creative, satisfying fulfilment and the degraded "unreal" feelings can be very powerfully present at one and the same time ' (1977 : 75). One of us had also shared this double experience and can affirm the meaningfulness of this statement. Caulfield sees this as the expression in everyday experience of the contradictions of use value production under capitalism. Her comment is also important because it brings the importance of feeling states into the debate.

Caulfield's assumption that use value production derives from 'a more humane past' (1977 : 75) may be oversimplified. Her notion that with use value social formations 'based on principles of reciprocity, egalitarianism, interdependence and autonomy of the individual' can exist is also somewhat doubtful because the evidence is that the concept of the autonomy of the individual arose with the development of exchange value and is closely associated with the rise of mercantilism and capitalism. Indeed, whether individual autonomy can co-exist with a merging into 'a solidary, intimate social group' is the nub of the problem, and one which affects all people but perhaps women particularly. The Marxist answer would be in the affirmative, indeed, only in communalism is individual self-fulfilment possible (cf. Lukes 1973 : 71). The important point however is that Caulfield draws attention to the presence in the family, even under capitalism, of communal, mutual values of worth which exist alongside the oppression and the denigration and are values to which plans for social re-formation should accord more space.

The economic structure of the contemporary family depends upon the ideology of love, service, and loyalty. The structure and the ideology have twin and contradictory consequences which at one and the same time put the woman in an oppressed and slave-like position and yet make possible valued and warm social relations. The task, not only for women, but for women and men, is to find a way of removing the oppression and retaining the valued aspects of mutuality and co-operation, not only in the family (or whatever set of social institutions may replace it) but also of extending these values to the society as a whole.

Given the odds, a great advance: how to go further?

It is our view that given the twin oppressions of state capitalism and of the domination of men in all major social, economic, and political institutions women have made remarkable advances over the past 200 years. But there is a long way yet to go. Ways have to be found of reconciling autonomy with co-operation, of retaining the positive values of mutual service while abolishing servitude. Organization, policy, and strategy have to be developed. The world will continue to be peopled by men and women, that is so long as we avoid a 'technological fix' in which

187

a male-dominated society determines that there should only be enough women for the reproduction of the species (Rose and Hanmer 1976). If that and similar threats connected with cloning can be avoided, the major problem remains. If we replace the slogan 'liberty, equality, and fraternity' by the more acceptable one of 'liberty, equality, and comradeship', what stance should women take in relation to formal political power? How can we achieve liberation at the same time as we retain and extend the valuable qualities of caring, of mutuality, of long-term attachment and loyalty that have been the best features of the family, patriarchal though it has been for aeons of history in the Western world?

To do this we have to recognize, first of all, as we have shown, that women are not equally and universally oppressed and, most importantly, that some women oppress other women. The oppressions of patriarchy, of capitalism, and of state power interlock and are mutually sustained and all have to be opposed. There is no doubt that sections of the working-class movement have been subverted to the maintenance of capitalism. Working-class leaders have not been able, so far, to use the positions of power they have achieved to make life more free and equal for all, either across classes or between sexes. This may be because socialist parties in now relatively minor states like Britain are not able to overcome the forces of international capitalism. It is also because those who achieve power are ambivalent about equality and comradeship. Whether women or men they are people who want to get on and do well and who are thus readily subverted. If a strategy of increasing the involvement of women in politics is to be followed, it is important, in our view, that the successful women should be kept closely in touch with a well-organized women's movement. Furthermore, we would agree with Rowbotham that such a movement must have a majority of working-class women (1973 : 126). Rowbotham is clear about the importance of organization for the liberation of women and in an extended essay (Rowbotham, Segal, and Wainwright 1979) argues that the women's liberation movement has contributed towards socialist as well as feminist liberation by creating ways of organizing in which leadership is much more widely dispersed than in left-wing organizations (p. 81). 'The

188

notion of organization in which a transforming vision of what is possible develops out of the process of organizing' (p. 146). In reviewing this work Elizabeth Wilson has drawn attention to the ambiguity in the feminist movement where some have wished for state power or the access to resources that power would give, while at the same time feminists have presented a radical critique of power relations. She asks 'What sort of power do [feminists] seek? In what way do we wish to make our mark on the world? Do we want to share in the world or do we simply want "women's sphere" to be given greater value? Or do we want to break out of these dichotomies altogether?' (1980 : 42–3).

These questions have to be answered. Yet, it would seem to us that if women wish to make changes in the societies they live in, they must seek and achieve power positions. It is essential that women should enter the political arena since the societies are all male-dominated, for men certainly cannot be relied upon to initiate or carry through the necessary changes. State socialist societies, communes, reformist and revolutionary societies have remained male-dominated. In advanced capitalist societies the older forms of women's power have been so far eroded and their private domain so utterly invaded by husband-father and state advisers, that women have no choice left to them but to seize an equal share of political power, notwithstanding all the odds which we have seen are stacked against us.

Participating in male-dominated capitalist states is a risky business, hence the importance of organizational backing. Furthermore, the strategy of encouraging women to gain power positions must clearly be linked with continuing discussions as to how we can achieve liberty, equality, and comradeship as con-crete not abstract values and link individual autonomy with collective action. Otherwise, in pursuance of this strategy, the sisterly and comradely goals of the women's movement will be subverted. In terms of its implications for women in relation to political institutions this discussion has been too long neglected. Socialists and feminists should put it high on their agenda.

Appendix

Table 1: Women parliamentary candidates and members: General Elections 1918-79

Year	Conservative women Cands.	MPs	Labour women Cands.	MPs	Liberal women Cands.	MPs	Others women Cands.	MPs	Total women Cands.	MPs	Total Both sexes Cands.	MPs
1918	1	0	4	0	4	0	8	1*	17	1*	1623	707
1922	5	1	10	0	16	1	2	0	33	2	1441	615
1923	7	3	14	3	12	2	1	0	34	8	1446	615
1924	12	3	22	1	6	0	1	0	41	4	1428	615
1929	10	3	30	9	25	1	4	1	69	14	1730	615
1931	17	13	36	0	5	1	4	1	62	15	1292	615
1935	19	6	33 2 Ind. Lab.	1	11	1	2	1	67	9	1348	615
1945	14 1 Ind. Cons.	1	41	21	20	1	11	1	87	24	1683	640
1950	28	6	42	14	45	1	11	0	126	21	1868	625
1951	25	6	41	11	11	0	0	0	77	17	1376	625
1955	33	10	43	14	14	0	2	0	92	24	1409	630
1959	28	12	36	13	16	0	1	0	81	25	1536	630
1964	23	11	33	18	25	0	8	0	89	29	1757	630
1966	21	7	30	19	20	0	9	0	80	26	1707	630
1970	26	15	29	10	23	0	21	1	99	26	1837	630
1974 Feb.	33	9	40	13	40	0	30	1	143	23	2135	635
1974 Oct.	30	7	50	18	49	0	32	2	161	27	2252	635
1979	31	8	51 2 Ind. Lab.	11	50	0	78	0	212	19	2572	635

* Irish Nationalist who did not take her seat.

Table 2: Women parliamentary candidates and members: General Elections 1918–79

Percentage Women

Year	Conservative Cands.	Conservative MPs	Labour Cands.	Labour MPs	Liberal Cands.	Liberal MPs	Others Cands.	Others MPs	All parties Cands.	All parties MPs
1918	0.2	0.0	1.1	0.0	1.0	0.0	2.0	0.9	1.0	0.1
1922	1.0	0.3	2.4	0.0	3.4	0.9	2.9	0.0	2.3	0.3
1923	1.3	1.2	3.3	1.6	2.6	1.3	3.8	0.0	2.4	1.3
1924	2.2	0.7	4.3	0.7	1.8	0.0	2.5	0.0	2.9	0.7
1929	1.7	1.2	5.3	3.1	4.9	1.7	6.9	11.1	4.0	2.3
1931	2.7	2.5	7.0	0.0	5.1	2.7	5.3	20.0	4.8	2.4
1935	3.3	1.4	6.3	0.6	6.8	4.8	3.8	9.1	5.0	1.5
1945	2.3	0.5	7.5	5.3	6.5	8.3	7.0	4.0	5.2	3.8
1950	4.5	2.0	6.8	4.4	9.5	11.1	7.0	0.0	6.7	3.4
1951	4.7	1.9	6.3	3.7	10.1	0.0	0.0	0.0	5.4	2.7
1955	5.3	2.9	6.9	5.0	12.7	0.0	3.6	0.0	6.5	3.8
1959	4.5	3.3	5.8	5.0	7.4	0.0	1.3	0.0	5.3	4.0
1964	3.7	3.6	5.2	5.7	6.8	0.0	6.0	0.0	5.1	4.6
1966	3.3	2.8	4.8	5.2	6.4	0.0	6.2	0.0	4.7	4.1
1970	4.1	4.5	4.6	3.5	6.9	0.0	8.3	14.3	5.4	4.1
1974 Feb.	5.3	3.0	6.4	4.3	7.7	0.0	8.0	4.3	6.7	3.6
1974 Oct.	4.8	2.5	8.0	5.6	7.9	0.0	8.3	7.7	7.1	4.2
1979	5.0	2.4	8.2	4.1	8.7	0.0	10.6	0.0	8.2	3.0

Table 3: *Women's membership of trade unions: 1926–76*

| Congress | Membership | | % of Total Women |
| | Women | Total | |
	(thousands)		
1926	447	4,366	10.2
1936	417	3,614	11.5
1946	1,242	6,671	18.6
1956	1,384	8,264	16.7
1966	1,747	8,868	19.7
1976	3,034	11,036	27.5

(Source: TUC 1977:4)

References

ABRAMS, P. and McCULLOCH, A., with S. ABRAMS and P. GORE (1976) *Communes, Sociology and Society*. Cambridge: Cambridge University Press.

ABRAMS, P., DEEM, R., FINCH, J., ROCK, P. (eds) (1981) *Development and Diversity: British Sociology, 1950–1980*. London: George Allen and Unwin.

ACWORTH, E. (1965) *The New Matriarchy*. London: Gollancz.

ARENSBERG, C.M. and KIMBALL, S.T. (1940) *Family and Community in Ireland*. Cambridge, Mass.: Harvard University Press.

ASAD, T. (1970) *The Kababish Arabs*. New York: Frederick Praeger.

AUSTIN, R. (1976) *Occupation and Profession in the Organization of Nursing Work*, Vols 1 and 2. Cardiff: The University of Wales, University College.

BACHRACH, P. and BARATZ, M.S. (1970) *Poverty and Power*. New York: Oxford University Press.

BAMBERGER, J. (1974) The Myth of Matriarchy: Why Men Rule in Primitive Society. In Z. Rosaldo and L. Lamphere (eds) *Women, Culture and Society*. Stanford, California: Stanford University Press.

BANKS, J.A. and O. (1964) *Feminism and Family Planning in Victorian England*. Liverpool: Liverpool University Press.

BANKS, O. (forthcoming) *Faces of Feminism*. Oxford: Martin Robertson.

BARKER, D.L. and ALLEN, S. (1976) *Sexual Divisions and Society: Process and Change*. London: Tavistock Publications.

BARTH, F. (1961) *Nomads of South Persia: Basseri Tribe of the Khameseh Confederacy*. Boston: Little Brown.

BEECHEY, V. (1977) Female Wage Labour in Capitalist Production. *Capital and Class* 3: 45–66.

—— (1978) Women and Production. In A. Kuhn and A–M. Wolpe (eds) *Feminism and Materialism*. London: Routledge and Kegan Paul.

194

—— (1979) On Patriarchy. *Feminist Review* **3**: 66–82.

BELL, C. and NEWBY, H. (1976) Husbands and Wives: the Dynamics of the Deferential Dialectic. In D.L. Barker and S. Allen *Dependence and Exploitation in Work and Marriage*. London: Longman.

BLACKSTONE, SIR WILLIAM (1753) *Sir William Blackstone's Commentaries on the Laws of England*.

BLONDEL, J. (1965) *Voters, Parties, and Leaders*. Harmondsworth: Penguin.

BLOOD, R.O. and WOLFE, D.M. (1960) *Husbands and Wives*. New York: The Free Press; London: Collier MacMillan.

BORLAND, M. (ed.) (1976) *Violence in the Family*. Manchester: Manchester University Press; New Jersey: Humanities Press.

BOTT, E. (1968) *Family and Social Network: Roles, Norms and External Relationships in Ordinary Urban Families*. London: Tavistock Publications (first published 1957).

—— (1971) *Family and Social Network: Roles, Norms and External Relationships in Ordinary Urban Families*. Second edition. London: Tavistock Publications.

BOWLBY, J. (1952) *Maternal Care and Mental Health*. Geneva: WHO.

BROOKES, P. (1967) *Women at Westminster*. London: Peter Davies.

BROWN, G.W. and HARRIS, T. (1978) *The Social Origins of Depression: A Study of Psychiatric Disorder in Women*. London: Tavistock Publications.

BROWN, J.K. (1975) Iroquois Women: An Ethnohistoric Note. In R.R. Reiter (ed.) *Towards an Anthropology of Women*. New York: Monthly Review Press.

BUJRA, M. (1978) Introductory: Female Solidarity and the Sexual Division of Labour. In P. Caplan and M. Bujra (eds) *Women United, Women Divided: Cross-Cultural Perspectives on Female Solidarity*. London: Tavistock Publications.

BYRNE, E.M. (1978) *Women and Education*. London: Tavistock Publications.

CAPLAN, P. (1978) Women's Organizations in Madras City, India. In P. Caplan and J.M. Bujra (eds) *Women United, Women Divided: Cross-Cultural Perspectives on Female Solidarity*. London: Tavistock Publications.

CARPENTER, M. (1977) The New Managerialism and Professionalism in Nursing. In M. Stacey, M. Reid, C. Heath, and R. Dingwall (eds) *Health and the Division of Labour*. London: Croom Helm; New York: Prodist.

CAULFIELD, M.D. (1977) Universal Sex Oppression? A Critique from Marxist Anthropology. In C. Nelson and V. Olesen (eds) *Catalyst* **10–11**: 8–36.

CHAMBERLAIN, M. (1975) *Fenwomen: A Portrait of Women in an English Village*. London: Virago, in association with Quartet Books.

CHANEY, E.M. (1973) *Women in Latin American Politics: The Case of Peru and Chile*. In A. Pescatello (ed.) Pittsburgh: University of Pittsburgh Press.

CIVIL SERVICE DEPARTMENT (1978) *List of Members of Public Boards of a Commercial Character as at 1 December 1978*. Cmnd 7417. London: HMSO.

CLARK, A. (1968) *Working Life of Women in the Seventeenth Century*. London: Cass (First published 1919).

CLARKE, E. (1978) *Sex Roles and Social Work*. Unpublished M.Sc. Thesis, Cranfield Institute of Technology.

COCKBURN, C. (1977) *The Local State: Management of Cities and People*. London: Pluto Press.

COLE, M. (1949) *Growing up into Revolution*. London: Longmans Green.

COLLIER, J. (1974) Women in Politics. In M.Z. Rosaldo and L. Lamphere (eds) *Women, Culture and Society*. Stanford, California: Stanford University Press.

CONSTANTINIDES, P. (1978) Women's Spirit Possession and Urban Adaptation. In P. Caplan and M. Bujra (eds) *Women United, Women Divided: Cross-Cultural Perspectives on Female Solidarity*. London: Tavistock Publications.

CUNNISON, I. (1966) *The Baggara Arabs: Power and Lineage in a Sudanese Nomad Tribe*. Oxford: Clarendon Press.

CURRELL, M.C. (1974) *Political Woman*. London: Croom Helm; New Jersey: Rowman and Littlefield.

DAHL, R.A. (1961) *Who Governs? Democracy and Power in an American City*. New Haven and London: Yale University Press.

DAVIDOFF, L. (1973) *The Best Circles: Society, Etiquette and the Season*. London: Croom Helm.

—— (1976) The Rationalization of Housework. In D.L. Barker and S. Allen (eds) *Dependence and Exploitation in Work and Marriage*. London and New York: Longman.

—— (1977) Power as an 'Essentially Contested Concept': Can It Be of Use to Feminist Historians? Unpublished paper to International Women's History Conference, University of Maryland, USA.

DEEM, R. (1978) *Women and Schooling*. London: Routledge and Kegan Paul Education Books.

DENNIS, N., HENRIQUES, F., and SLAUGHTER, C. (1974) *Coal Is Our Life: An Analysis of a Yorkshire Mining Community*. London: Tavistock Publications (first published 1956).

DOBB, M. (1947) *Studies in the Development of Capitalism*. New York: New World Paperbacks.

DOUGLAS, M. (1970) *Natural Symbols; Explorations in Cosmology*. New York: Random House, Pantheon.

DUVERGER, M. (1955) *The Political Role of Women*. Paris: UNESCO.

EHRENREICH, B. and ENGLISH, D. (1979) *For Her Own Good: 150 years of the Experts' Advice to Women*. London: Pluto Press.

EISENSTEIN, Z.R. (1979) *Capitalist Patriarchy and the Case for Socialist Feminism*. New York, London: Monthly Review Press.

ENGELS, F. (1960) *The Origin of the Family*. London.

—— (1969) *The Conditions of the Working Class in England*. London: Panther.

EPSTEIN, C.F. (1980) Women and Power: The Role of Women in Politics in the United States. In C.F. Epstein and R.L. Coser (eds) *Access to Power: Cross-National Studies of Women and Elites*. London: George Allen and Unwin, pp. 124–40.

EPSTEIN, C.F. and COSER, R.L. (1980) *Access to Power: Cross-National Studies of Women and Elites*. London: George Allen and Unwin.

ETTORE, E.M. (1980) *Lesbians, Women and Society*. London, Boston, and Henley: Routledge and Kegan Paul.

FAWCETT, M.G. (1912) *Women's Suffrage: A Short History of a Great Movement*. London: T.C. and E.C. Jack.

FERGUSON, S. (1977) Labour Women and the Social Services. In L. Middleton (ed) *Women in the Labour Movement: the British Experience*. London: Croom Helm.

FINKELSTEIN, C.A. (1980) Women Managers: Career Patterns and Changes in the U.S. In C.F. Epstein and R.L. Coser (eds) *Access to Power: Cross-National Studies of Women and Elites*. London: George Allen and Unwin.

FIRESTONE, S. (1971) *The Dialectic of Sex: The Case for Revolution*. New York: Bantam.

FOGARTY, M., RAPOPORT, R., and RAPOPORT, R.N. (1971a) *Women in Top Jobs: Four Studies in Achievement*. London: George Allen and Unwin.

—— (1971b) *Sex, Career and Family*. London: George Allen and Unwin.

FOLSOM, J.K. (1948) *The Family and Democratic Society*. London: Routledge and Kegan Paul.

FRANKENBERG, R. (1957) *Village on the Border*. London: Cohen and West.

—— (1976) In the Production of Their Lives, Men? . . . Sex and Gender in British Community Studies. In D.L. Barker and S. Allen (eds) *Sexual Divisions and Society: Process and Change*. London: Tavistock Publications.

FRANSELLA, F. and FROST, K. (1977) *On Being a Woman: a Review of Research on How Women See Themselves*. London: Tavistock Publications.

FULFORD, R. (1976) *Votes for Women*. London: White Lion (previously published 1958).

GALLIE, W.B. (1955–56) Essentially Contested Concepts. *Proceedings of the Aristotelian Society* **56**: 167–98.

GARDINER, J. (1976) A Case Study in Social Change: Women in Society. In *Reform or Revolution?* Open University D302 Units 31–32. Milton Keynes: The Open University Press.

GAUDRY, M. (1929) *La Femme Chaonia L'Aurès*. Paris: Geuthner.

GERTH, H.H. and WRIGHT MILLS, C. (1948) *From Max Weber: Essays in Sociology*. London: Routledge and Kegan Paul.

GILLESPIE, D.L. (1972) Who Has Power? The Marital Struggle. In H.P. Dreitzel *Family, Marriage, and the Struggle of the Sexes*. Recent Sociology No. 4. New York: Macmillan.

GODELIER, M. (1975) Modes of Production, Kinship and Demographic Structures. In M. Bloch (ed.) *Marxist Analysis and Social Anthropology*. New York: Wiley.

GOODE, W. (1963) *World Revolution and Family Patterns*. New York: Free Press.

GOOT, M. and REID, E. (1975) *Women and Voting Studies: Mindless Matrons or Sexist Scientism?* London and Beverly Hills: Sage Publications.

GRAHAM, H. (1979) Prevention and Health: Every Mother's Business: A Comment on Child Health Policies in the 70s. In C.C. Harris (ed.) *The Sociology of the Family: New Directions for Britain*. Sociological Review Monograph 28, Keele: University of Keele.

GREG, W.R. (1877) *Literary and Social Judgements* Vol. II. Fourth edition. London: Trübner and Co.

GRIGG, J. (1979) *The Observer*. London: 25 November.

GUARDIAN, THE (1979) 5 November.

HAMILTON, R. (1978) *The Liberation of Women*. London: George Allen and Unwin.

HANSARD (1867) *Hansard's Parliamentary Debates*, Vol. 187, col. 825–26. London.

HARDY, T. (1974) *The Mayor of Casterbridge*. London: Macmillan.

HARRELL–BOND, B.E. (1969) Conjugal Role Behaviour. *Human Relations* **22** (1): 77–91.

HARRIS, C.C. (1969) *The Family*. London: George Allen and Unwin.

—— (1977) Changing Conceptions of the Relation between Family and Societal Form in Western Society. In R. Scase (ed.) *Industrial Society: Class, Cleavage and Control*. London: George Allen and Unwin.

HARRISON, B. (1978) *Separate Spheres, The Opposition to Women's Suffrage in Britain*. London: Croom Helm.

HARTMAN, M. and BANNER, L.W. (1974) *Clio's Consciousness Raised: New Perspectives on the History of Women*. New York: Harper Torchbacks.

HAWKES, J. (1958) *Dawn of the Gods*. London: Chatto and Windus.

HILLS, J. (n.d.) Participation by Women in the Labour and Conservative Parties. Mimeo. University of Essex.

HUBERT, J. (1974) Belief and Reality: Social Factors in Pregnancy and Childbirth. In M.P.M. Richards (ed.) *The Integration of a Child into a Social World*. Cambridge: Cambridge University Press.

HUNT, P. (1978) Cash Transactions and Household Tasks. *Sociological Review* **26**, 3, New Series, August. Keele, University of Keele.

—— (1980) *Gender and Class Consciousness*. London and Basingstoke: Macmillan.

IGLITZIN, L.B. and ROSS, R. (eds) (1976) *Women in the World: A Comparative Study*. Oxford: Clio Books.

IREMONGER, L. (1961) *And His Charming Lady*. London: Secker and Warburg.

JAMES, S. (1972) Introduction to M. Dalla Costa and S. James, *The Power of Women and the Subversion of the Community*. Bristol: Falling Wall Press.

JAQUETTE, J. (1976) *Female Political Participation in Latin America*. In L.B. Iglitzin and R. Ross (eds) *Women in the World: A Comparative Study*. California and Oxford: Clio Press.

KAMM, J. (1966) *Rapiers and Battleaxes*. London: George Allen and Unwin.

KELSALL, K. (1955) *Higher Civil Servants in Britain from 1870 to the Present Day*. London: Routledge and Kegan Paul.

KERR, M. (1958) *The People of Ship Street*. London: Routledge and Kegan Paul.

KLEIN, J. (1965) *Samples from English Cultures*. London: Routledge and Kegan Paul (2 vols).

KLEIN, R. and LEWIS, J. (1976) *The Politics of Consumer Representation*. London: The Centre for Studies in Social Policy.

KORDA, M. (1978) *Power: How to Get It, How to Use It*. London: Hodder and Stoughton.

KUHN, A. and WOLPE, A-M. (1978) *Feminism and Materialism: Women and Modes of Production*. London, Henley and Boston: Routledge and Kegan Paul.

LABOUR PARTY, THE (1972) *Discrimination Against Women*. Report of a Labour Party Study Group. London: The Labour Party.

—— (1979) *Women Candidates May 1979 – General Election*. London: The Labour Party National Conference of Women. Mimeo.

LAND, H. (1976) Women: Supporters or Supported? In D.L. Barker and S. Allen (eds) *Sexual Divisions and Society: Process and Change*. London: Tavistock Publications.

LASLETT, P. (1971) *The World We Have Lost*. London: Methuen.

LAWRENCE, E. (1977) The Working Women's Charter Campaign. In M.

199

Mayo (ed.) *Women in the Community*. London: Routledge and Kegan Paul.

LEACOCK, E. (1975) Class, Commodity and the Status of Women. In R. Rohrlich-Leavitt (ed.) *Women Cross-Culturally: Change and Challenge*. The Hague: Mouton.

LERNER, D. (1979) *The Passing of Traditional Society: Modernizing the Middle East*. Glencoe: The Free Press.

LICHTENSTÄDTER, I. (1935) *Women in the Aiyam Al-'Arab*. London: The Royal Asiatic Society.

LIDDINGTON, J. and NORRIS, J. (1978) *One Hand Tied behind Us: the Rise of the Women's Suffrage Movement*. London: Virago.

LIPSHITZ, S. (ed.) (1978a) *Tearing the Veil: Essays on Femininity*. London: Routledge and Kegan Paul.

—— (1978b) The Personal is Political: The Problem of Feminist Therapy. *M/F* 2: 22–31.

LITTLEJOHN, J. (1963) *Westrigg: the Sociology of a Cheviot Parish*. London: Routledge and Kegan Paul.

LUKES, S. (1973) *Individualism*. Oxford: Basil Blackwell.

—— (1974) *Power: a Radical View*. London and Basingstoke: Macmillan.

LUPTON, T. and WILSON, S.C. (1973) The Social Background and Connections of 'Top Decision Makers'. In J. Urry and J. Wakeford (eds) *Power in Britain*. London: Heinemann Educational Books.

McCARTHY, M. (1977) Women in Trade Unions Today. In L. Middleton (ed.) *Women in the Labour Movement: the British Experience*. London: Croom Helm.

McCOWAN, S. (1975) *Widening Horizons: Women and the Conservative Party*. London: Conservative Political Centre.

McGREGOR, O.R (1957) *Divorce in England*. London: Heinemann.

McNAMARA, J.A. and WEMPLE, S. (1974) The Power of Women through the Family in Medieval Europe: 500–1100. In M. Hartman and L.W. Banner (eds) *Clio's Consciousness Raised*. New York: Harper Torchbacks.

MACKIE, L. and PATTULLO, P. (1977) *Women at Work*. London: Tavistock Publications.

MAHER, V. (1976) Kin, Clients and Accomplices: Relationships among Women in Morocco. In D.L. Barker and S. Allen (eds) *Sexual Divisions and Society: Process and Change*. London: Tavistock Publications.

MANN, M. (1973) *Consciousness and Action among the Western Working Class*. London: Macmillan.

MARCUSE, H. (1979) T.V. broadcast interview by Brian Magee, BBC 27.1.79 (first broadcast 1978).

MARKS, P. (1976) Femininity in the Classroom: An Account of Changing Attitudes. In J. Mitchell and A. Oakley, *The Rights and Wrongs of*

Women. Harmondsworth: Penguin.

MARSHALL, T.H. (1963) Citizenship and Social Class. In *Sociology at the Crossroads*. London: Heinemann.

—— (1969) Reflections on Power. *Sociology* **3**(2).

MARX, E. (1967) *Bedouin of the Negev*. New York: Praeger.

MARX, K. (1954) *Capital*. Vol. 1. London: Lawrence and Wishart.

—— (1973) *Grundrisse. Foundations of the Critique of Political Economy*. Harmondsworth: Penguin, in association with *New Left Review*.

MAYS, J.B. (1954) *Growing up in the City*. Liverpool: Liverpool University Press.

MERCK, M. (1978) The City's Achievements: The Patriotic Amazon-omachy and Ancient Athens. In S. Lipshitz (ed.) *Tearing the Veil*. London: Routledge and Kegan Paul.

MERNISSI, F. (1975) *Beyond the Veil: Male-Female Dynamics in a Modern Muslim Society*. Cambridge, Massachusetts: Wiley, Schenkman.

MIDDLETON, C. (1979) The Sexual Division of Labour in Feudal England. *New Left Review* **113–14**: 147–68.

MIDDLETON, L. (1977) Women in Labour Politics. In L. Middleton (ed.) *Women in the Labour Movement*. London: Croom Helm.

MILBURN, F. (1976) *Women as Citizens: A Comparative Review*. London: Sage Publications.

MILL, J. (1937) *An Essay on Government*. Cambridge: Cambridge University Press.

MILLER, J.B. (1976) *Towards a New Psychology of Women*. Harmondsworth: Penguin.

MILLETT, K. (1977) *Sexual Politics*. London: Virago.

MITCHELL, H. (1977) *The Hard Way Up* (ed. G. Mitchell). London: Virago.

MITCHELL, J. (1971) *Woman's Estate*. Harmondsworth: Penguin.

—— (1976) Women and Equality. In J. Mitchell and A. Oakley *The Rights and Wrongs of Women*. Harmondsworth: Penguin.

MOGEY, J. (1956) *Family and Neighbourhood*. London: Oxford University Press.

MOHSEN, S. (1970) Legal Status of Women among the Awlad 'Ali. *Anthropological Quarterly* **40**(3). Reprinted in L. Sweet (ed.) *Peoples and Cultures in the Middle East*. New York: Natural History Press.

MOORE, K. (1974) *Victorian Wives*. London: Allison and Busby.

MYRDAL, A. and KLEIN, V. (1956) *Women's Two Roles: Home and Work*. London: Routledge and Kegan Paul.

NELSON, C. (1973) Women and Power in Nomadic Societies of the Middle East. In C. Nelson (ed.) *The Desert and the Sown: Nomads in the Wider Society*. Research Series No. 21, University of California, Berkeley: Institute of International Studies.

—— (1974) Private and Public Politics: Women in the Middle Eastern

World. *American Ethnologist* **1**(3): 551–65.

NELSON, C. and OLESEN, V. (1977) Veil of Illusion: a Critique of the Concept of Equality in Western Feminist Thought. In *Catalyst* **10–11**: 8–36.

NEWLAND, K. (1975) *Women in Politics: A Global Review*. Washington D.C.: Worldwatch Institute.

NOVARRA, V. (1980) *Women's Work, Men's Work: The Ambivalence of Equality*. London: Marion Boyars Publications Ltd; New Hampshire: Marion Boyars Inc.

NOWOTNY, H. (1980) Women in Public Life in Austria. In C.F. Epstein and R.L. Coser (eds) *Access to Power: Cross-National Studies of Women and Elites*. London: George Allen and Unwin.

OAKLEY, A. (1974a) *The Sociology of Housework*. Oxford: Martin Robertson.

—— (1974b) *Housewife*. London: Allen Lane.

—— (1976) Wisewoman and Medicine Man: Changes in the Management of Childbirth. In J. Mitchell and A. Oakley, *The Rights and Wrongs of Women*. Harmondsworth: Penguin.

—— (1979a) The Failure of the Movement for Women's Equality. *New Society*, 23 August: 392–4.

—— (1979b) *Becoming a Mother*. Oxford: Martin Robertson.

O'BRIEN, E. (1978) *Mother Ireland*. Harmondsworth: Penguin.

Observer, The, 4 April 1976.

PAHL, J.M. and PAHL, R.E. (1971) *Managers and Their Wives*. London: Allen Lane.

PANETH, M. (1944) *Branch Street*. London: George Allen and Unwin.

PANKHURST, R.K.P. (1954) *William Thompson (1775-1853) Britain's Pioneer Socialist, Feminist and Cooperator*. London: Watts.

PANKHURST, S. (1977) *The Suffragette Movement*. London: Virago.

PEHRSON, R. and PEHRSON, J. (1966) The Social Organization of the Marri Baluch. Viking Fund Publication. *Anthropology* **43**: 59.

PESCATELLO, A. (ed.) (1973) *Female and Male in Latin America: Essays*. Pittsburgh: University of Pittsburgh Press.

PETERS, E. (1966) Consequence of the Segregation of the Sexes among the Arabs. Paper delivered at the Mediterranean Social Science Conference, Athens. Mimeo.

PINCHBECK, I. (1977) *Women Workers and the Industrial Revolution 1750–1850*. London: Cars.

POLSBY, N.W. (1963) *Community Power and Political Theory*. New Haven and London: Yale University Press.

POWER, E. (1975) *Mediaeval Women* (ed. M.M. Postan). Cambridge: Cambridge University Press.

PROSS, H. (1980) Women in Management in West Germany. In C.F. Epstein and R.L. Coser (eds) *Access to Power: Cross-National Studies of*

Women and Elites. London: George Allen and Unwin.

RAMELSON, M. (1972) *The Petticoat Rebellion: A Century of Struggle for Women's Rights*. London: Lawrence and Wishart (first published 1967).

RAPOPORT, R. and RAPOPORT, R. (1971) *Dual-Career Families*. Harmondsworth: Penguin Books.

REITER, R.R. (ed.) (1975) *Toward an Anthropology of Women*. New York and London: Monthly Review Press.

RENDEL, M. (1977) The Contribution of the Women's Labour League to the Winning of the Franchise. In L. Middleton (ed.) *Women in the Labour Movement*. London: Croom Helm.

RIGBY, A. (1974) *Communes in Britain*. London: Routledge and Kegan Paul.

ROSALDO, M.Z. (1980) The Use and Abuse of Anthropology: Reflections on Feminism and Cross-Cultural Understanding. *Signs: A Journal of Women in Culture and Society* 5(3) Spring.

ROSALDO, M.Z. and LAMPHERE, L. (1974) *Women, Culture and Society*. Stanford, California: Stanford University Press.

ROSE, H. and HANMER, J. (1976) Women's Liberation, Reproduction and the Technological Fix. In D.L. Barker and S. Allen (eds) *Sexual Divisions and Society: Process and Change*. London: Tavistock Publications.

ROSS, J.F.S. (1953) Women and Parliamentary Elections. *British Journal of Sociology* 4(1): 14–24.

—— (1953) *Elections and Electors*. London: Eyre and Spottiswoode.

ROSSER, C. and HARRIS, C. (1965) *The Family and Social Change*. London: Routledge and Kegan Paul.

ROWBOTHAM, S. (1973) *Women's Consciousness, Man's World*. Harmondsworth, Penguin.

—— (1974a) *Women, Resistance and Revolution*. Harmondsworth, Penguin.

—— (1974b) *Hidden from History: 300 Years of Women's Oppression and the Fight against It*. London: Pluto Press.

ROWBOTHAM, S., SEGAL, L., and WAINWRIGHT, H. (1979) *Beyond the Fragments: Feminism and the Making of Socialism*. London: Merlin Press.

ROYAL COMMISSION ON LOCAL GOVERNMENT IN ENGLAND (1969) *Radcliffe-Mand Report*. London: HMSO.

RUETHER, R.R. (1974) *Religion and Sexism: Images of Women in the Jewish and Christian Traditions*. New York: Simon and Schuster.

RUSH, M. (1969) *Selection of Parliamentary Candidates*. London: Nelson and Sons.

RUSKIN, J. (1902) *Sesame and Lilies*. Chicago: Homewood.

SACHS, A. and WILSON, J.H. (1978) *Sexism and the Law: A Study of Male*

Beliefs and Legal Bias in Britain and the United States. Oxford: Martin Robertson.

SAFILIOS–ROTHSCHILD, C. (1969) Family Sociology or Wives' Family Sociology? A Cross-Cultural Examination of Decision Making. *Journal of Marriage and the Family* **31**(2): 290–301.

—— (1970) The Study of Family Power Structure: A Review 1960–1969. *Journal of Marriage and the Family* **32**: 539–52.

SAIFULLAH–KAHN, V. (1976) Purdah in the British Situation. In D.L. Barker and S. Allen (eds) *Dependence and Exploitation in Work and Marriage*. London: Longman.

SANDRAY, P. (1974) Female Status in the Public Domain. In M.Z. Rosaldo and L. Lamphere (eds) *Women, Culture and Society*. Stanford. California: Stanford University Press.

SEABROOK, J. (1973) *The Unprivileged*. London: Penguin.

SHARMA, U. (1978) Segregation and Its Consequences in India. In P. Caplan and J.M. Bujra (eds) *Women United, Women Divided: Cross-Cultural Perspectives on Female Solidarity*. London: Tavistock Publications.

SMITH, D. (1974) Women, the Family and Corporate Capitalism. In M. Stephenson (ed.) *Women in Canada*. Toronto: New Press.

SOPHIA (1975) *Woman Not Inferior to Man*. London: Brentham Press.

Spare Rib (1977) Working for the Union. No. 59, June.

SPINLEY, B. (1954) *The Deprived and the Privileged*. London: Routledge and Kegan Paul.

STACEY, M. (1960) *Tradition and Change: A Study of Banbury*. London: Oxford University Press.

—— (1965) *Lower Swansea Valley: Housing Report*. Swansea: University College of Swansea. Mimeo.

—— (1981) The Division of Labour Revisisted, or Overcoming the Two Adams. In Abrams, P., Deem, R., Finch, J., and Rock, P. (eds) *Development and Diversity: British Sociology, 1950–1980*. London: George Allen & Unwin.

STACEY, M. and PRICE, M. (1979) The Law Is Not Enough. Paper presented to the BSA Annual Conference, Warwick. Mimeo, University of Warwick.

STACEY, M. and STACEY, R.J. (1979) Personal communication.

STANWORTH, P. and GIDDENS, A. (eds) (1974) *Elites and Power in British Society*. Cambridge: Cambridge University Press.

STEVENS, P. (1973) *Marianismo:* the Other Face of *Machismo* in Latin America. In Ann Pescatello (ed.) *Female and Male in Latin America: Essays*. Pittsburgh: University of Pittsburgh Press.

STONE, L. (1977) *The Family, Sex and Marriage in England 1500–1800*. London: Weidenfeld and Nicolson.

204

STONE, M. (1976) *The Paradise Papers: The Suppression of Women's Rites*. London: Virago.

STORR, M.S. (1932) *Mary Wollstonecraft et le Mouvement Féministe dans la Littérature Anglaise*. Paris: Les Presses Universitaires de France.

STOTT, M. (1978) *Organization Woman: The Story of the National Union of Townswomen's Guilds*. London: Heinemann.

STRACHEY, R. (1978) *The Cause: a Short History of the Women's Movement in Great Britain*. London: Virago (first published 1928).

STURGES-JONES, E. (ed.) (1975) *Women in Politics*. London: Conservative Central Office.

SULLEROT, E. (1977) Background Paper: The Changing Roles of Men and Women in Europe. In U.N. Seminar *The Changing Roles of Men and Women in Modern Society: Functions, Rights and Responsibilities*, Vol. II. New York: United Nations.

TAYLOR, B. (1978) The Woman-Power: Religious Heresy and Feminism in Early English Socialism. In S. Lipshitz (ed.) *Tearing the Veil: Essays on Femininity*. London: Routledge and Kegan Paul.

THOM, B. (1980) Women in International Organizations: Room at the Top. The Situation in Some United Nations Organizations. In C.F. Epstein and R.L. Coser (eds) 1980 *Access to Power: Cross-National Studies of Women and Elites*. London: Allen and Unwin.

THOMPSON, D. (1976) Women and Nineteenth-Century Radical Politics: a Lost Dimension. In J. Mitchell and A. Oakley (eds) *The Rights and Wrongs of Women*. Harmondsworth: Penguin.

THOMPSON, E.P. (1963) *The Making of the English Working Class*. Harmondsworth: Penguin.

THOMPSON, W. (1825) *An Appeal of One Half of the Human Race, Women, against the Pretension of the other Half, Men, to retain them in Political, and thence in Civil and Domestic Slavery*. London: Longmans Hurst Rees.

TRADE UNION CONGRESS (1977) *Women Workers, 1977, Report on the 47th Annual Conference of Representatives of Trade Unions Catering for Women Workers*. London: TUC.

—— (1979) *Women Workers, 1979, Report on the 49th Annual Conference of Representatives of Trade Unions Catering for Women Workers*. London: TUC.

URRY, J. and WAKEFORD, J. (1973) *Power in Britain*. London: Heinemann Educational Books.

VALLANCE, E. (1979) *Women in the House: a Study of Women Members of Parliament*. London: The Athlone Press.

WADE, J. (ed.) (1835) *The Black Book*. London: Effingham Wilson.

WALLIMAN, I., ROSENBAUM, H., TATSIS, N. and ZITO, G. (1980) Misreading Weber: The Concept of 'Macht'. *Sociology* **14**(2).

WEBER, MARIANNE (1975) *Max Weber: A Biography* translated by H. Zohn. New York: Wiley.

WEBER, M. (1978) *Economy and Society* (ed. G. Roth and C. Wittich). Berkeley, Los Angeles, London: University of California Press.

WEBSTER, P. (1975) Matriarchy: A Vision of Power. In R.R. Reiter (ed.) *Toward an Anthropology of Women*. New York and London: Monthly Review Press.

WEINBAUM, B. (1978) *The Curious Courtship of Women's Liberation and Socialism*. York, Philadelphia: South End Press.

WESTERGAARD, J. and RESLER, H. (1975) *Class in a Capitalist Society: A Study of Contemporary Britain*. New York: Basic Books.

WHITEHEAD, A. (1976) Sexual Antagonism in Herefordshire. In D.L. Barker and S. Allen (eds) *Dependence and Exploitation in Work and Marriage*. London: Longman.

WILLIAMS, G. (1945) *Women and Work*. London: Nicholson and Watson.

WILLIAMS, W.M. (1956) *The Sociology of an English Village: Gosforth*. London: Routledge and Kegan Paul.

WILSON, E. (1977) *Women and the Welfare State*. London: Tavistock Publications.

—— (1980) Beyond the Ghetto: Thoughts on *Beyond the Fragments – Feminism and the Making of Socialism*, by Hilary Wainwright, Sheila Rowbotham and Lynne Segal. *Feminist Review* 4: 28–44.

WOLLSTONECROFT, M. (1975) *A Vindication of the Rights of Women* (ed. M. Krammick). Harmondsworth: Penguin (first published in 1792).

WOLPE, A–M. (1978) Education and the Sexual Division of Labour. In A. Kuhn and A–M. Wolpe *Feminism and Materialism: Women and Modes of Production*. London, Henley, and Boston: Routledge and Kegan Paul.

Woman's Own, 17 February 1979.

WOODHAM–SMITH, C. (1950) *Florence Nightingale*. London: Constable.

WOOTTON, B. (1967) *In a World I Never Made: Autobiographical Reflections*. London: George Allen and Unwin.

WORSLEY, P. (1964) The Distribution of Power in Industrial Society. In Sociological Review Monograph No. 8, *The Development of Industrial Societies*, Keele: University of Keele.

WRONG, D. (1979) *Power: Its Forms, Bases and Uses*. Oxford: Basil Blackwell.

YOUNG, M. and WILLMOTT, P. (1973) *The Symmetrical Family: a Study of Work and Leisure in the London Region*. London: Routledge and Kegan Paul.

ZARETSKY, E. (1976) *Capitalism, the Family and Personal Life*. London: Pluto Press.

Name index

Numbers in italics indicate an entry in the bibliography

Subject index